Seen

Female Entrepreneurs Share Their Story of How They Stepped Into Their Passion, Purpose & Power

A Collaboration Hosted by
Katherine Massey

SEEN

Female Entrepreneurs Share Their Story of How They Stepped Into Their Passion, Purpose & Power

ISBN: 978-1-7398027-0-7

Published in the United Kingdom

Hosted by: Katherine Massey

Cover & interior design by: Michelle Catanach

VQ Academy

TEAM AUTHOR UK
Publishing with you

To Craig Massey, my childhood love.

At age 11 we started our romance; 35 years later, you still believe in me when many did not, including myself. I love you today and more tomorrow.

Your girl, Katherine.

Foreword

I was approached by Katherine who asked me if the proceeds of *Seen* could go to 'Milestone Mums'. I was completely overwhelmed and grateful that such inspiring women felt that we should be given the proceeds. Self-belief is something that I haven't been comfortable with over the years but having others believe in me and my charity helps me to believe in myself.

I was a mum who had a mental illness whilst I was pregnant and after the baby was born. It took a very long road to recovery to get me to where I am today. Even now, there are days when I feel overwhelmed and unsure of how to deal with challenges. I soon realised after having my baby that there was no support for mothers. There was nowhere to go to talk and say that being a parent really sucks at times (but I wouldn't change it for the world). I decided to create a safe space for mothers to bring their children and talk, make friends and feel less isolated. After three years of running 'Milestone Mums', we are making big differences. Mums are talking, we know it's OK not to be OK and that there most definitely is no shame in having struggles.

This book will help, encourage and inspire other mums to believe that mental health doesn't have to be a reason to give up. Sometimes, your breakdown can be your breakthrough and seeing other people who have experienced similar problems is comforting.

Seen truly aligns with my ethos in giving others hope at a time when they are in despair. Women need to be seen. We need to be acknowledged that we are not a machine that just 'gets on with it'. Mums are important, mums matter and mums need to be valued. There are always people there for the baby but no one is there for the mum...

Until now.

Sarah Finlay

Founder, Milestone Mums

Connect With Sarah:

Facebook: www.facebook.com/milestonemums1

Email: milestone_mums@outlook.com

Contents

Introduction

I knew what I needed and wanted to do. It was the start of the 2020 pandemic and my business was turned upside down. After some soul-searching, manifesting and training, I developed an online business and membership group as the 'Visibility Queen'. Women were drawn to my purpose, which was to help female entrepreneurs stand proud in their purpose, while guiding, encouraging and facilitating them to be Seen.

Working with so many wonderful women – all with amazing stories and backgrounds – it was time for me to create a platform where they could come together, share their experiences, while letting their courage inspire future generations.

This collection is a book of hope, courage and reflection. It's been emotional for them and for me. I feel I have lived every day, week and month as they've shared their vulnerability and fear of being seen.

Each woman experienced unique challenges in their past that ultimately framed their future. It helped lead them to their passion, and what has now become their life's purpose.

I'm confident these women now recognise the power that storytelling has to not only heal and overcome, but to rise above. What further stories will they be emboldened to share, I wonder. I believe there will be more to come. But for now, please enjoy their wisdom in their own words.

They stepped into their power for you ... knowing it was finally time to be *Seen*.

Much love and light,

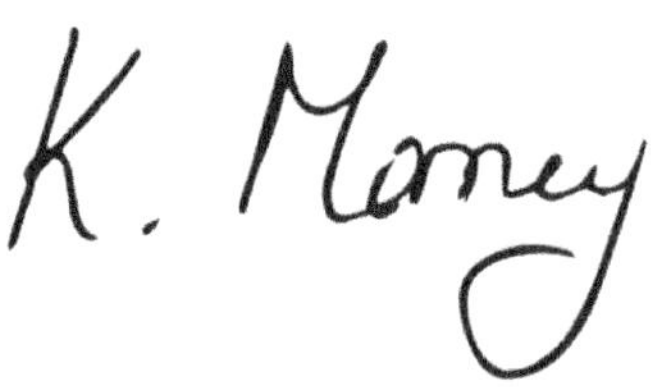

Katherine Massey

Visibility Queen

When I Was Scared of People

By Jen Griffiths

'It's okay to be scared. Being scared means you're about to do something really, really brave.' ~ Anon

Have you ever been scared of your own shadow? Ever been afraid of everyone and everything at the same time? The fear of judgement was rooted so deep into my very being that I'd lost all sense of what it meant to simply live.

Even a diagnosis, counselling, a mindfulness course and CBT (cognitive behaviour therapy) didn't help. No one had any solutions and support was lacking because I didn't know how to ask for it. As a student, I struggled to make lasting friendships and would get clingy and insecure. Over time, this resulted in me becoming scared to message 'friends' and they'd end up dropping off the radar and losing touch. As a working adult, I got stuck in zero-hour contracts because I was terrified of change and had no aspirations or ambitions. I was anxious at my own wedding; I struggled at every single job interview (except the one where I didn't care because I thought I was a lost cause) and then I became quite possibly the only piano teacher in the area who was scared of playing in public! I was a nobody, and due to several years of bullying I had got used to being invisible. I blended so far into the background that no one noticed me. For a while, it didn't bother me. Over time, however, I became a doormat and a wallflower which was often frustrating. I'd do anything for anyone but often received nothing back. I let people take the credit when it was me who put most of the work in – I was too weak to stand up to anyone. It wasn't until lockdown in 2020 that I started to find my way out of the dark hole I'd lived in for so many years. Many describe lockdown as the darkest year of their life, but I can honestly say it was the year of light for me! Let's rewind a bit...

Losing Myself

The very notion of finding my 'power' was a terrifying concept. Initially, through my lifelong anxiety disorder, I was convinced I was a lost cause and hopeless! Most of all, I was so afraid of being judged that I would never take any opportunities or risks. Other (more confident) people would walk straight in and take the opportunities while I watched in the distance wishing it could have been me.

Why did I think I was a lost cause?

Because, in my eyes, I was a failure.

I was a failure at writing because the teachers didn't think much of it. I was a failure because I couldn't knit; I could only crochet. I was a failure at sport because I wasn't allowed to do what the boys were doing. I was a failure at acting because I was better in the recorder band. I was a failure because I would fall apart at exams. I was a failure because I allowed myself to get bullied. I was a failure because I never 'grew out' of being a gamer. I was a failure because I didn't get any 'A' grades at A Level. I was a failure because I didn't get a 1st degree (I got a 2:1). I was a failure because I didn't become a schoolteacher. I was a failure because I was a pianist who was too shy to play to anyone. I was a failure because I got stuck on zero-hour contracts. I was a failure because I joined an 'MLM' (multi-level marketing) company.

Did this mean that I had failed at life in general? Of course not. But it's what I believed.

People had worn me down for so many years with their opinions and expectations that I started to believe I was a failure as a person and would never amount to anything. As a result, I ended my education with no ambition, no aspirations ... nothing. I had no idea what I truly wanted to do. I'd been pushed in a certain direction for too long and I wanted it to stop...

Except I didn't.

I met the love of my life at age 21. I was a passionate soul. I was deeply romantic but also terrified of displaying it in case I was seen as weak or hopeless. I struggled to express emotion unless I wrote it down so, in my teens, I turned to poetry. I loved writing. I'd write stories too. No one ever read them but they were in a journal of sorts. Along with my daily diary entries and my 'best days' diary, I was always writing something.

Growing up, I could never be myself. If I wasn't trying to fit in I was being invisible on purpose so as not to get noticed by the bullies. This continued well into adulthood. I was scared of everyone. I hated being the centre of attention. I couldn't keep up with fashion – I was the kid wearing leggings and a woolly jumper in year seven when all the other girls were head-to-toe in denim! (I eventually got my denim but by then everyone was in miniskirts with leggings.) In my later teens I became a 'mosher' because my friend was one, blending in with her and therefore 'succeeding' at being invisible ... again.

Who *was* I? I had no idea. I thought it wasn't socially acceptable to be myself – an adult gamer who likes collecting plushies and a 'secret' pianist who has perfect pitch and a specialism in sight-reading. The two things didn't really work together even though I'd met plenty of gamers who were also musicians. Most of those who I had met were shy too, though many came out of their shell (partly) thanks to the gaming community I built with my husband off the back of our wedding. I thought that I, too, was finally coming out of my shell. Despite a five-year vendetta against me, where our community did nothing but flourish, the only way was up! I was finally getting comfortable with being a host. I could host whole tournaments and attend national events (I was socially anxious for most of them). I made myself known to other gaming groups as the 'founder' that wanted to talk to people rather than play the games. I just wanted to network! Except, in those days, that meant saying 'Hi' nervously, then hoping the conversation would make itself.

The biggest growth of the community was during my worst professional years. When I took on a role as maternity cover it was a great overall experience, however, it didn't sort the anxiety out. The job took me out of my comfort zone but I always felt like an outcast. I wasn't true to myself. Again, I was just trying to fit in. I wanted to be liked. I was very sensitive to the 'vibes' though. If I sensed someone didn't like me, I'd distance myself and they would trigger my anxiety, leaving me permanently 'on edge'.

A private office job after the maternity cover destroyed what little confidence I had left. I was bullied, accused of being a 'loser' for liking video games and told that I should get a life! (Running a whole community isn't seen as having a life because apparently a gamer isn't entitled to have a life.) I never revealed that I played the piano. What was the point? The company wasn't interested in me as a person. They just wanted someone who did the job. No personality needed! Without that 'final' experience of bullying, however, I may never have made the decision to become self-employed.

A Wake-Up Call

I was like a fish out of water in the new world of self-employment. I finally started to think that I could be myself. *I'm a musician. I'm a pianist. Chase the piano things!*

Then I got pregnant.

Everyone says you lose your friends when you have a baby. I'd spent years building up the gaming community and gained friends off the back of it. I was terrified of losing it all. So, I fought hard from day one. I kept my identity – I didn't want to 'just' be a mum. I was a pianist. I was a gamer! I barely coped though. I was a zombie one day and having complete blanks the next, sleep deprived but still expected to function. How we got through it as new parents I'll never know – we just did! If friends went off and did stuff without me, it would trigger my anxiety and I'd wonder why I wasn't invited. *Was it because I was now a mum?* It was the very thing I was fighting against but it added to my heightened anxiety.

I fought so hard to keep my identity. I didn't realise I was losing myself. By 2019, I was teaching piano, accompanying a small local choir and playing at the local National Trust site. I was keeping my head above water but only just. I was miserable. People picked up on the negative energy and, towards the end of the year, I felt so lonely. My husband had all but frozen me out. I felt like I was only invited to places out of pity.

Getting ill in 2019 was a massive wake-up call. *You can't go on like this. This is not a life. This is a shell. You've failed again. Just give up.* Mentally I *had* given up. I didn't care what I was doing to myself. I merely existed to be there for everyone else. I tried to remember self-care; I went to pilates once a week ... It evidently wasn't enough.

In September 2019, the world came crashing down around me. *STOP! Who am I? Why am I doing this?* I ended up in hospital because of gallbladder problems. I had a breakdown and realised that I'd relied on junk food and sugar for far too long. It had to stop. But mentally, I didn't have the strength. I sobbed to my husband. I had no idea how to fix myself. What I did know was this: I loved my child, I loved my husband, but I didn't love me!

By the end of 2019, I'd essentially scared myself into losing weight and eating more carefully. I was terrified of hospitals, so the prospect that I might have to go back if I triggered an illness scared me into eating more mindfully. I changed my whole lifestyle that winter. Christmas 2019 was probably one of my lowest points. My anxiety was sky-high and I was on edge 24/7. I was even scared to eat my Christmas dinner that year! The best way for me to communicate my feelings was by writing. So, that Christmas, I wrote my husband a 'letter'. Reflecting back, that was the first step I needed to address my anxiety disorder head on. I hated using my disorder as an excuse, but when behaviour is fuelled by anxiety it is the only explanation. My husband understood. That 'letter' allowed us to seek understanding of each other on a deeper level.

Finding My Power

When lockdown hit in March 2020, I was still a pianist and gamer, however, I faced losing the 'piano' bit. Everything moved online. I got overwhelmed quickly. *Who am I? I don't know anymore. I'm supposed to be everything to everyone. I'm sinking again...*

I joined a network marketing company (MLM) and, little did I know, this would be the best decision I ever made.

I struggled for the first few months, doing what can only be described as 'plodding' along, but one thing I learnt early on was the need to be consistent. *Never give up! You'll get there one day!* After six months, I started to see a way forward. I had new confidence. I was constantly challenging myself to step out of my comfort zone, I was building the foundations again. I effectively started from scratch. I never thought about what I was actually doing but I realised that lockdown was presenting itself as the best chance in my life to GROW, to take control and stop the anxiety disorder running and ruining my life! I grabbed all of the opportunities that were thrown my way. Sometimes I signed up for too many things and got overwhelmed, but even that was a lesson! Every day I was learning something new, soaking it up like a sponge. I always loved learning but most of the things I'd learnt as an adult were fairly useless (being a note taker in many subjects has that effect). Now was the time to learn proper life skills and, most importantly, master emotional intelligence and resilience.

Nine months in and I started to feel more established. Various challenges pushed me to think about what I stood for. *Do I actually know what I want from life? What are my core values? What is my mission? What is my 'why'?* I'd never answered those questions before or set serious goals. It all unfolded, step by step, one challenge or training at a time. I wrote reams and reams of notes. I learnt and absorbed everything! I picked 'Tropic Pianist Gamer' as my personal 'brand' after being inspired by the 'Singing Scentsy Lady'... I'm a Tropic Ambassador, I'm a Pianist, I'M A GAMER! 'Three' is my magic number. I've believed that throughout life, so at that point everything aligned. I'd found my 'magic three'!

By Christmas 2020, I had worked out who I was, who I wanted to be, and what I stood for. It was such a liberating feeling and I no longer feared being judged. After spending so many years being scared of pretty much everything and everyone, a weight lifted from my shoulders.

Despite trying to fit in at school and growing up, despite trying to blend in and not be noticed, I always liked being different. I've always been creative; I love using my imagination. I love storytelling. I love being my unique self. People tell me that I look genuinely happy in photos they see of me now. I finally found my power. I finally feel like I can stand up and be counted!

In hindsight I realise that lockdown presented the opportunity to take my anxiety disorder by the horns, shake it violently, and see what fell out. Hopefully, if I shake it enough, it'll be in so many pieces that it won't know how to fit back together again. Essentially, I needed to 'deconstruct' the anxiety disorder to find my purpose.

Tropic Pianist Gamer is my brand. It is truly me. It is truly unique.

I'm also a blogger and amateur poet. Because I love being a storyteller, and I'll always be creative.

I'm no longer afraid of judgement. I'm no longer afraid of bullies. I'm no longer afraid of trolls ... and I'm no longer afraid of my parents!

I've taken control, I'm standing in my power and I'm owning it!

About the Author

Jen Griffiths is known as The Tropic Pianist Gamer. She always liked to be different but being bullied all the way through childhood and into adulthood meant that she hid away for years, afraid of being judged.

Having had anxiety since the age of 13 and only being diagnosed at the age of 27, Jen stepped into her power in her 30s, finally taking back control of her life. Embracing the badge of Anxiety Warrior, Jen rediscovered her identity and allowed her unique self to shine through. With one of her hidden passions being writing, she set out to inspire others with her stories and poetry!

Connect With Jen:

Website: www.tropicpianistgamer.co.uk
Instagram: www.instagram.com/tropic.jen

Finally! I'm Emotionally Free

By Lisa Preston

'Much of the beauty of light owes its existence to the dark.'
~ Brené Brown

I first started to experience mental ill-health at 11 years old – I just didn't know it back then.

Growing up, I did everything I thought I was meant to to be successful. I kept my head down, focused and did well at school. I went to university and then started a career that was meant to be for life, following in my dad's footsteps by joining the police. But by my early 30s, everything I had worked towards was lost.

Disarmed and Disillusioned

The police force was not how I imagined it would be. I had to fight for the career progression I was aiming for and when I had children, I was put between a rock and a hard place. It was impossible for me to continue a career alongside motherhood.

After having my first daughter in 2011, I went back to work on an agreed working pattern. We lived 200 miles from family, I needed to work full-time and childcare wasn't accessible for shift working. It was very difficult. I worked 12-hour nights and took care of our baby during the day – I wasn't just 'new-parent' sleep-deprived. I was surviving on two hours' sleep per day for four to five days a week and then 'regular' broken sleep around a baby on the other days. I did this for two years, up until I was 36 weeks pregnant with my second child.

After my second daughter, I developed postnatal depression (PND). The ins and outs of how that looked for me are too in-depth for this chapter, but on top of dealing with that, it also became the beginning of the end for my career.

I should have been able to (and wanted to) have both a career and raise a family. I knew I'd have to make sacrifices in those early years, but I needed help to facilitate childcare needs, just like they did for other working mothers. I was still a valuably trained officer; I was hard working and competent in my role. But that didn't matter in the end. The force I served in was ill-educated, archaic and had no idea how to support a working mother with PND.

I didn't tell them I had PND when I first went back – I was too scared to. The force appallingly mismanaged me during the loss of my dad in 2007 and so I knew how it was going to go if I told them. Things were initially 'fine'. I was sort of coping – putting on a smile, masking just how tired I was and muddling along, powered by caffeine.

Then it started to go wrong. The Force was demanding more of me in ways I couldn't meet and that didn't fit the parameters of my contract or agreed hours, and eventually I had to declare I was taking medication … I was bang on the mark about how things were going to go. My medical information was shared way beyond acceptable parameters, and I was forced into a dark and difficult corner.

Over a period of the next 6-12 months, I was slowly oppressed, bullied, harassed and destroyed to the point where I became a shadow of my former self. I was passed from person to person. I had to go into work each day and explain my PND, why I worked the hours I did, what medication I was on, why this meant I couldn't do certain training as a result, and why I couldn't travel 100 miles away for seven weeks to do it. I was reliving it all every day and I wasn't sleeping much in between. I was made to feel incompetent; my vulnerability was wide-spread knowledge, and I felt shame like I never had before. The word 'FAILURE' was in neon lights flashing at me every waking moment - and as I wasn't sleeping much at all, you can imagine how things were spiralling out of control.

My body and mind were catapulted into a permanent state of 'fight' and adrenaline was pumping through me constantly. I would sob at the thought of going to work. I'd be bombarded with emails while at home, researching and writing proposals and reports to explain everything over and over about how I *could* facilitate all they needed from me with just a few reasonable adjustments, and then I would head to work for a 12-hour night shift. My husband would come home and, in the half hour we had before I left, I'd have to 'gear up' and pep talk myself ready for another fight. I'd put my war paint on to cover the deep purple eye bags, red raw eyes and the greying skin tone of my face. It was a mask I increasingly resented having to wear.

I planned, prepared, researched, reached out, fought back, pleaded, cried, and begged for help. I put forward business case proposals, but never once did they agree to meet me halfway. Never. In the end, it came down to a choice of their way – or leave. I should add that now, five years on, TWO of the proposals I put forward are now in place as working roles within the organisation.

Through all this, my PND escalated, and I developed general anxiety disorder. I was struggling to go out, paranoid that I was being followed by supervisors from work. I would physically tremble from exhaustion and all my senses were completely distorted. I found it hard to even do a supermarket shop without feeling over-stimulated and exhausted. I cancelled plans and found it difficult to experience reality – I'd fallen apart.

From Walking the Beat to Downbeat

In August 2015, I woke up one morning and something felt very wrong. I opened my eyes and turned on the lights, but it still seemed dark. Everything was shadowed and dull and I had no peripheral vision; I could see what was in front of me, but it was like I had blinkers on.

After many trips to hospital, it was determined that I'd suffered from optic neuritis, a swelling of the optic nerve, and there was a chance that the damage was permanent. I'd also developed painful migraines. I was sent for brain scans and blood tests and was told that it could be a precursor for multiple sclerosis. Luckily, that was ruled out and the symptoms were put down to stress.

Going on sick leave gave work the final piece of ammunition they needed to edge me out. Even whilst I was poorly, they persisted and pushed. I had supervisors from work turning up on my doorstep unannounced and I was being pressed for a return-to-work date. Because I couldn't give one, I was placed on a procedure to 'manage me back to work' – even though I was on doctor's certified sick. Work called hearings that I was physically unable to attend but they filed it as misconduct and put me into a disciplinary procedure. I felt I had no other choice; I finally replied to their barrage of emails with my resignation.

It was like a weight had been lifted; I had become so flattened: physically, emotionally, and mentally, that walking away from that job, in short, saved my life.

I remained poorly, in pain, unable to see properly (my remaining eyesight rapidly reducing) … and I'd just halved our household income. We had a mortgage in the southeast of England and, although we had some savings, they wouldn't last long. My husband put in for a vacancy in the Midlands and, although it took a long time to grant and then to sell our house, 12 months later, we moved. I watched all our hard-earned savings disappear and even had to dip into the savings accounts we'd started for the kids. I felt so guilty.

In Summer 2017, we arrived in Shropshire and worked hard to get our lives back on track. I put my efforts into making the house a home, helped the kids transition into a new nursery and school and supported the hubby with his new job.

I was still yet to figure out where I belonged and, no matter how relieved I was to finally leave, I grieved the loss of my job. I was angry, lost and so deeply sad; I'd lost my professional identity. It might not have lived up to my expectations, but it was still what I had wanted to do with my life. Without it, I didn't know what else to do. None of my skills seemed to translate into the outside world a decade on.

Relieving the immediate stress allowed my body to start healing physically and my vision started to improve but I was left with anxiety, depression, and paranoia, as well as a deep sense of self-loathing.

With little other option, I attempted self-employment, seeing it as the only way to try and make a living around our home life. I was first introduced to the idea in 2014 with a network marketing business. It started off well, but when the leadership and business structure changed, I realised it wasn't for me. I didn't want the boundaries of success to be dictated to me again – I'd just left that behind. What it did help me with was social networking and the idea that maybe I could create something of my own.

I began to try some business ideas out. I played to what I thought were my strengths, did some courses and learning but couldn't find anything that 'fit'. I was stumbling through and my anxiety meant I didn't have the capacity to advertise and put myself out there.

My eldest daughter had developed some difficulties too. She was showing signs of mental ill-health and, after a lot of research and turbulent periods, we tied her symptoms to a neuro-immune condition called PANS PANDAS. In its simplest form, it is brain inflammation because of an infection in the body and it exhibits itself as psychological symptoms. Things were intense. My daughter was in and out of school, up and down health wise, her mental health took a battering and it greatly added to the unpredictability of life.

Everything was overwhelming, I was flailing. I couldn't find a way to bring money in; I felt unskilled, useless, a rubbish mother – I couldn't help my own daughter. I felt that I'd failed at everything I had tried my hand at and that no one liked me. I was living in this new place and felt so isolated.

I quite literally didn't recognise myself anymore. I had no idea where the Lisa I once knew had gone. I used to be strong and feisty. I'd laugh and joke my way through everything. I was fun to be around, and I quite liked that about myself. I could take everything in my stride -- but not anymore.

I became so ambivalent about life; I was exhausted, confused, frightened and lonely. It affected everything – work, relationships, my confidence. I didn't feel strong anymore and completely ran out of the capacity to bottle things up, to compartmentalise or deal with everything going on. In such a short period of time, so many different people and circumstances had let me down or chopped away at me, and my soul was left with next to nothing to give. It took all the strength I had to shut it away from the kids so I could be there for them, but I wasn't functioning well at all.

I couldn't clear the head space to even organise and clean the house properly, or to remember birthdays. I couldn't complete work projects and I was committing to the wrong things. Things I thought I could do but when it came to it, seemed like an unclimbable mountain. It's like I was weighed down under crushing water with my head bobbing along the surface fighting for breath.

I was too tired to handle anything more than trying to survive. I was living with a consuming voice in my head telling me how utterly rubbish I was. I began berating myself for being lazy, unmotivated, and feeling stuck. I wasn't living anymore; I was responding to life with survival strategies.

I never had any thoughts to end my life but I did give up on it. I felt I was here to raise my children and so stopped dreaming for myself – I had no other sense of purpose but them. I attended a workshop for some self-development, thinking it would be the answer. There was an exercise to write a list of things you like about yourself. I'll never forget the feeling that flooded me – I couldn't think of a single nice thing to write about myself. I closed the book and sat with a heavy pulse throbbing in my ears. There was no room to hide, everyone saw. They all tried to help, were encouraging, kind and compassionate, but I still couldn't do it.

I carried around the weight of all those broken pieces of me for a long time and it wasn't until the world slowed down during the first lockdown of 2020 that I was able to take stock.

Restoring Order

Before the pandemic, I had been searching long and hard for ways to help my daughter with all she was going through and was introduced to a wonderful lady who taught a programme for mental health support. I went and I listened; it was so simple, yet effective, that I wanted to learn more. So, I learned to teach it myself and began to realise that my passion lay in mental health and helping others.

I'd never want to take away the seriousness and impact of the pandemic, but for me it was a time when I did a lot of thinking and learning. During those gentle days where nothing more was expected of us than to stay home, I began, gradually, healing my own open wounds.

We did face challenges too – we lost income, went months without seeing loved ones – but I knew this time that it wasn't my fault and that helped me realise that some things can be beyond our control. When you're stuck in a spiral of your own mental ill health, there's no perception to help you see that.

I had time to think and I did some writing to try and work things out. I started being creative and used it to launch a hand-made jewellery business which took off beautifully and I found a place in the online world with it.

I was reading, taking courses, spending time with family and playing games. Despite not being able to see friends and family that lived further away, we were more connected than ever because we all made the extra effort.

I was refilling myself with everything that I'd put to one side or forgotten about to prioritise the kids or because I was in survival mode. I'd disappeared so far into myself that I'd forgotten all the things which brought me joy and helped me to be me.

I decided to enrol on a course to become a hypnotherapist and psychotherapeutic counsellor and started seeing my own therapist to get some professional help in solidifying the foundations I'd started building for myself.

I know now I'm on the right path. I'm coaching, creating, learning, growing, and starting to dream towards a future again. I started the perfect-fit job that I absolutely LOVE and it gets me out of the space where being self-employed can leave you feeling isolated and lonely.

There are lots of components that make up me and I've managed to arrange them into a way that works for me and my family – I never thought I'd find that again.

I'm working towards a new, fulfilling future and finally have my sense of purpose returned. I'm happy and I can see ahead; I can say nice things about myself again and I don't carry the burden of failure anymore – I'm ready to accept any changes if and when they come.

I do live a very privileged life and I've never not been grateful for all I have, but mental ill health can strike anyone at any time and have a profound impact on all areas of your life. What happened at work wasn't my fault and by taking a more objective view of my experience I've been able to see that.

It's important for anyone to know that you can reach this point too by taking a step back and finding the help you need. You don't need to keep living the same narrative.

It is up to you to determine what success means for you. It's not determined by income, bank balance, house size, cars, clothes, followers or anyone else's definition – I'm still building my businesses, but they are wonderfully successful as they are at this moment in time because I determine they are.

Having personal therapy has been like turning on a light; facing my pain has helped me start to heal it. I hadn't grieved properly for any of the losses in my life and needed to. Grief doesn't just show up when someone close to you dies. It comes up when you lose a job or face big changes. I was grieving my dream, my career, the person I was before, and all this sat on top of the unprocessed grief of losing my dad at age 23, which is another story – one that precedes this one.

I've spent all my adult life running from my story, trying to stay one step ahead and outrun my demons with fresh starts, a positive mindset and hope, but I was just plastering over the cracks. The truth is, if you don't learn to understand the root causes of your pain, your story may catch up with you.

That's why I'm now training to be a therapist and why mental health coaching is my calling – so I can help you realise it too, help you heal, help you determine your own success, find your inner peace, and see ahead again ... *Step by Step.*

About the Author

Lisa Preston is a multiple business owner, boutique manager, writer, student, charity volunteer, mother of two, wife, and owner of three dogs. She is the creative designer behind a hand-made jewellery brand that grew from the 2020 lockdown and is now stocked in a number of establishments across the Midlands.

Lisa is a qualified reflexologist, hypnotherapist, mental health coach and is training to become a psychotherapeutic counsellor, as well as a volunteer for the charity PANS PANDAS UK. She is determined to contribute towards normalising the language used around mental health and is passionate about supporting children's mental wellbeing as they navigate an ever-changing and increasingly complicated world.

Connect with Lisa:

Linktree: linktr.ee/lisah_preston
Facebook: @stepbystep.wellbeing
Instagram: @walkwildjewellery

Drunk Warrior

By Becky Field

'Most people, even though they don't know it, are asleep, they marry in their sleep, they breed children in their sleep, they die in their sleep without waking up.' ~ Anthony de Mello[(1)]

'You fucking did that to him … YOU! You are a fucking drunk.'

The shame rose from the base of my feet and surged up, up, up, all through my body.

I woke up.

This was the start of the day that changed my life.

I sat there feeling totally humiliated, shamed, shocked, confused and so desperately lonely. I couldn't have been any further from the door of the treatment centre room, the door which I desperately wanted to run through.

'You're selfish, so fucking selfish, you're nothing but a drop-down drunk.'

I was 30 years old, incredibly successful as a further education tutor, and yet, here I was, a drop-down, selfish drunk. I was three months, nine days sober on the day that changed my life. Full of ego, full of what I now know to be called *'euphoric recall'* or, in plain English, *'bullshit'*. I was utterly convinced that I was the victim, that I was the one hard done to and that *'if you had my life you would drink too'*.

That day changed *everything*.

Thankfully, the onslaught lasted five or ten minutes and its impact continues as I write this, over 15 years later. I wanted to run. I couldn't do this. *How dare they speak to me that way. Me, an educated lecturer and a professional woman, how dare they!*

A kind man I recognised from AA then said to me outside, 'What's the alternative, Becky?'

On the afternoon of 'the day that changed my life', we were gathered in the very same room that I had endured the onslaught … and I hid. Sandwiched between two people I had never met, I dared not look at anyone. The shame was huge … *I* had done that to him.

We were each given a folded piece of paper and told not to open it.

'You each have a piece of paper and on that piece of paper it will either say 'alive' or 'dead',' said the counsellor. My heart began to thud. *You can die from this?* The counsellor went on to describe the statistics (at that time in 2006): one in four people make it in recovery.

One in four make it ... ALIVE, ALIVE ... ALIVE.

One in four ... my dad, my brother, me, my brother.

1, 2, 3, 4...

One in four...

My heart beat faster and harder than I'd ever known. *One in four, ALIVE, ALIVE ... ALIVE, one in four.*

I began to pray, willing my piece of paper to say 'alive' and, as each person was asked to read their paper, my heart beat heavier and heavier, faster and faster. *One in four ... ALIVE, ALIVE ... ALIVE. One in four.*

'DEAD.' My eyes shot up. The counsellor recalled how people who had gone through the treatment centre had died. Vomiting and choking on their own vomit, falling downstairs while drunk, alcoholic seizures ... *ALIVE, ALIVE ... ALIVE ... One in four.* Swallowed their own tongue in blackout, drink driving ... *ALIVE, ALIVE ... ALIVE ... One in four.* Cirrhosis of the liver, alcoholic hepatitis ... *ALIVE ... ALIVE ... One in four.*

As they came nearer and nearer to me, my heart nearly burst out of my chest. I felt weak and unable to breathe. *Please let it be me, please let me be the one.*

'Becky?'

My fingers trembled as I opened up the tiny piece of paper. *Let it be me, ALIVE, one in four …* my heart … 'ALIVE,' I read.

I had never before, or have since, experienced the intensity of wanting something that much. Of wanting to live that much. Of wanting sobriety that much. And the crazy thing was I didn't think I was 'that bad' – I had no idea!

You see, I was good at lying. I was dishonest. I had spent 12 years convincing myself I was OK so I totally and utterly believed it.

I was blinded by alcohol and the impact on all aspects of my life. That day that changed my life was also the day I had no choice but to wake up – the onslaught woke me up.

I woke up to find I was desperately lonely having isolated myself and my partner because of my behaviour. I woke up angry without knowing at whom or why but mainly hating myself. I woke up to baffled work colleagues who had borne the brunt of my frustration and anger. And I woke up to so much detachment from reality that it was difficult to differentiate the truth from the lies.

But the worst thing was that I woke up to the horrific consequences of the effects of living with a 'functioning alcoholic' or 'chemically dependent person'. In short, living with a selfish, inconsiderate, drop-down, often aggressive drunk.

I don't say this for effect, I say it as a fact. Shame has no place in my life today, and neither does buttering this illness up or prettying descriptions to more socially accepted labels. My name is Becky and I am an alcoholic and in active recovery today.

If you are reading this and questioning whether you have a problem with drink, let me tell you this: you do. If you didn't, you wouldn't even question it. So, how was I convinced?

Control and Choice

'Can you stop and stay stopped?' Chris asked. I was at my first AA meeting on September the 16th, 2005. I *could* stop, you see. I was a professional – of course I could stop. I stopped when I was too ill to drink. I stopped when I had completely embarrassed myself. I stopped when I was in the doghouse … but I couldn't *stay* stopped.

There was always an excuse to drink; always someone to blame for picking up a drink and always someone I was angry at because I didn't get my way.

There was also always a reason to celebrate. A birthday, a wedding, a christening, a Tuesday, a Friday … You get my point. When I was no longer in the doghouse, or I had convinced myself *again* that 'I wasn't that bad', I would start again. This behaviour was repeated time and time again, convincing myself that I couldn't possibly have a problem.

'Can you control it once you start to drink?' Chris asked.

At the end of my drinking my behaviour was unpredictable. I was a loose cannon. People would give me bullets and I would willingly fire them. I had little consideration for anybody once I was drinking.

On my last drunken night, I threatened a man I had never met with a pint pot in a pub. I was in a blackout. I had no recollection at all. I had no idea how I had got home, where my phone was, or how I had paid to get home. This wasn't the first time in such a state, but it was the first time that I had lost control to the point of threatening violence and risking imprisonment. All out of my control.

Anyone reading this who thinks alcoholism is a choice is incorrect. Why would anyone choose to hurt their loved ones? Why would anyone choose to put themselves in sexually vulnerable positions due to lack of control? Why would anyone choose to slowly kill themselves and destroy the wellbeing of others in the process? Why would anyone choose death over being alive?

Drinking is a symptom. I could have chosen drugs, food, sex, gambling, cleaning, chocolate, you name it. Once I put the drink down, the work then began.

Recovery meant changing everything – this is where the need to stop becomes questionable to so many that the urgency diminishes. These are life or death decisions for someone like me. Nearly 16 years in and I'm telling you: the commitment to recovery wavers when you realise it has absolutely nothing to do with drink. It is nothing to do with what was done to you, and has everything to do with you *changing* you, *knowing* you, and ultimately *loving* you.

Changing You

'I can't possibly do this for 12 weeks. What about Alan?' I said to the counsellor, desperate to get out of the onslaught.

'You've not been there for him for 12 years; another 12 weeks won't make any difference.'

I was cocooned in treatment for 12 weeks initially. No friends, no family, absolutely nothing or no one associated with drinking. 'Change your playground, change your playmates' they said. The truth was that I had alienated my playmates through my behaviour, and those who remained soon went when I stopped buying the drinks.

I had to go over my life with Alan, the deep consequences and effects my drinking had on him and our relationship, our lives, his happiness, our happiness. Our life which appeared to be normal.

You will often read an exercise where people write their life story when going into treatment. My *War and Peace* was 48 pages long. I was applauded after I read it out, but not positively applauded for its well-written prose or dramatic detail (remember, I was full of ego). Rather, I was applauded for the total sob story and blame game described in such masterly detail. It was literally a fantasy.

I was then asked to rewrite the story based on my relationship with Alan. My thoughts went back to 'the day that changed my life'. *I did that to him … I did that to him.* I began to write. Eighteen pages later, I woke up further. I was then asked to take out any 'blame statements' before I read it out. This was a life-changing exercise.

I had to take full responsibility for me and my life. If I was to recover fully, I had to stop looking to blame and be accountable for my actions, my behaviour, my words. I had to put things right.

Right with my partner, my family, my employer, and finally, myself.

Thankfully, I was able to put things right with my mum before she died on the day that I was six months sober. March 16th, 2006.

I had just shared what I believed to be my biggest consequence in a consequence session. I was called out of the treatment room, the same room where the onslaught happened in January, to find Alan waiting for me downstairs.

My mum was in hospital, and it wasn't good. She was 65.

I grabbed my phone. 2.13pm. We had to get to Southport. *Please let me make it. Please let me make it. She will be OK if I get there.* I couldn't drive, I couldn't think. *Please let me make it. Please let me make it.* As we drove into the hospital entrance, I saw my dad and my brother outside. *Why weren't they with Mum? No, no, no, NO …* I fell into my dad's arms.

The biggest consequence of my drinking was that I wasn't with Mum when she died because I was in a treatment centre for alcoholism. Again, I don't say this for effect. I say this because it is a fact. I was 30 years old and yet I believed 'I wasn't that bad'.

Knowing You

I know today that I suffer from a mental illness and that I am mentally and bodily different from those 'normal folks' that can drink normally. I have a head that tells me I can drink and a body that tells me I can't.

In the process of recovering, I have got to know that every alcoholic is selfish, inconsiderate, dishonest and frightened. After years of using writing as part of my recovery, alongside self-reflection and personal development, I know I can still be all those things. The difference today is that I know how to channel these for good. *One in four … ALIVE, ALIVE … ALIVE … One in four.*

I know today that both my parents saw me sober before they died. My dad shortly followed my mum after my third year of recovery. They both knew and saw that I was **alive.**

As part of my healing, I had to ask my dad to look me straight in the eyes and tell me he loved me. I knew he did, but I needed him to tell me. I learned to ask for what I needed, and I learned to ask for what people needed from me.

I know today that recovery is a gift and that it should be appreciated. I know that I can choose at any time to drink by simply stopping growing, stopping owning my shit and reverting back to blaming others and playing the 'poor me' game. *Poor me, poor me, pour me another.*

In 2014, the thought of driving my car into a bridge appealed to me. I was eight years sober, my life was externally perfect, but I was ill. I was burnt out mentally, emotionally, and spiritually. I was empty. I had lost sight of what it meant to be *free* in recovery. Although the thought of a drink was never present, who in their right mind considers driving themselves into a bridge to stop the pain?

Coaching saved my life. It reminded me that I still wanted to be ALIVE. It gave me back my desire to live. I started on my coaching journey through group coaching. The power of being with men and women who felt the same as me was life-changing.

Week by week, life was breathed into me through wonderful exercises which made me re-evaluate my life. I discovered that I was out of balance. Every aspect of my life had been neglected as I neglected my own wellbeing.

I woke up!

Recovery is about change. I changed everything … again.

I changed who I surrounded myself with, I changed the way I spoke to myself, I changed the things I did that took away my joy and I quit putting others before myself.

I knew I wanted more; I knew I deserved more. My passion for coaching was influenced by my wonderful coach Hannah, to whom -- along with my friend Mel who kindly told me to 'go to the doctor, sweetie' -- I owe my life.

Although statistics now state that there were 5,698 alcohol specific deaths in the UK in 2018, I am so glad, selfishly, to still be the *one in four*.

Loving You

I love myself enough today to keep my piece of paper with 'ALIVE' written on it in a box beside my bed.

I love myself enough today to know that my 28-year relationship with my partner is on solid ground. It's not perfect, but it's solid.

I love myself enough today to be ruthless about myself and my recovery. My emotional and mental sobriety comes above everything and everyone.

I love myself enough today to have a black belt in boundaries which is my signature within all aspects of my life. These boundaries are non-negotiable, unshakable, and purely and utterly selfish.

My passion in my coaching business, working with service-based business owners is to give you permission to create non-negotiable and unshakeable boundaries for your mental and emotional wellbeing. You can be a mum, daughter, brother, dad, sister, partner, granddaughter, drunk, druggie, addict, parent of an addict, entrepreneur, cleaner, baker, butcher, candlestick maker ... I really don't care. My mission is to make you care about *you*.

So, is it time to take back control? Is it time to stop blaming others? Is it time to face up to your responsibility?

I was a drop-down drunk. I was selfish, dishonest, inconsiderate, and terribly frightened. I was dangerously anti-social and angry. 'An alcoholic in his cups is an unlovely creature' [2] says the *Alcoholics Anonymous Big Book,* but today I consider myself to be a 'lovely creature'. A formidable force in the coaching world, a warrior in business, and a warrior for mental health, sobriety, and for service-based business owners who inevitably put others before themselves.

My slogan is 'there is always a solution' which also comes from a chapter from the AA big book *Alcoholics Anonymous.* That chapter saved my life, and I am hoping (without ego) that this chapter will go towards saving the life (or lives) of the person(s) who reads it. I am hoping that someone is you!

References

1) de Mello, A. (2000). *Awareness*. Bantam Doubleday Dell.

2) Alcoholics Anonymous Big Book (4th ed.). (2002). Alcoholics Anonymous World Services. Page 16

About the Author

Becky Field is a coach, mentor, hypnotherapist and practitioner of NLP & Time Line Therapy® – with a black belt in boundaries. Becky believes that everyone's life can be transformed through coaching, letting go of all the bollocks that holds us back, and facing everything with courage – or a sledgehammer!

She knows that every small business owner deserves more. With an unshakeable belief that there is always a solution, Becky will help you develop your own black belt in boundaries and a wonderfully balanced life through one-to-one or group coaching.

She is a food lover, a dog lover, a bright spark and a breath of fresh air!

Connect With Becky:

Facebook: www.facebook.com/westfieldcoaching
Instagram: www.instagram.com/westfieldcoaching
LinkedIn: www.linkedin.com/in/westfieldcoaching
Twitter: twitter.com/westfield_coach

Embracing the Change

By Laura Coote

My darling you are strong, you will come through this, and you will have learnt so much about yourself! Embrace the journey, allow it to become part of your new chapter.

I'll never forget her words.

'Ok, Mrs Coote, so there are two babies in here. I'm just checking to see if there are any more.' *Jesus H Christ, did she just say there are two and she's looking for more? How on earth will I cope? How will I manage a toddler and being pregnant, never mind having twins?* That moment is one I will never forget. I never knew it was possible to feel such excitement, elation, fear, anxiety and panic all at once.

My eldest was 22 months when the twins were born. 'It's a boy,' said the doctor. Then the second twin came and they cheered, 'It's another boy!' I was delighted. I loved being a mum to my first little boy and, as long as they were all healthy and safe, that was all we cared about.

The Fog

How am I here again?

Sat in this same spot, on the cold kitchen floor, heavy, exhausted and lost. I could feel the cold kitchen tiles. I liked the feeling of the coldness on my legs – it made me feel alive and grounded. Most of all, it helped me bypass the overwhelming feeling of guilt.

If I could have five more minutes of quiet, maybe I'd be OK. I'd pray that those five minutes could help me get the energy I needed to get through the day.

The fog is thick today; it engulfs me.

It is the most confusing feeling. I know I'm in it, I can see it, I can feel it … but I can't get out of it.

I fight so hard against it but that makes me even more tired. So, I do the only thing I can … I collapse into it.

The guilt is unbearable. Guilt that I have what so many other people want yet here I am, sitting on this floor again, with no energy to get up.

So, I sit. I pray for the quiet to continue and allow another few minutes of the day to pass.

The silence is deafening. Our house is set back from the road so there is no noise, no distractions, no passing traffic. It's either complete silence or absolute chaos.

While I'm praying for silence, I am also very aware that I want to hear my children, I want to know they're OK!

I find it incredibly difficult to comprehend how much I can love them yet wish for bedtime to come quickly so that I can breathe my silent air for a few hours between feeds. I know that when bedtime comes I'll want my children with me because the love I have for them is immeasurable.

I want to enjoy everything about them. I want to listen to them breathe and do all the cute stuff that every other 'earth mother' seems to be doing with their children. Yet here I am, sitting on this bloody floor again, thinking.

Thinking about how I can be better, how I can do this better, how I can enjoy this more … You see, today is a bad day, the fog is thick. Though some days are good. It feels like a rollercoaster that I want to get off but there is no emergency button, no one to come and take off my seatbelt and set me free.

I'm annoyed at myself, angry that I can't pull myself out of this fog. It's strangling me – I'm exhausted. I keep looking back at the 'me' before the fog and I want to be that fun-loving person again – the happy one, the one who has all her shit together and lives her life for the 'right here, right now'!

I've always lived like that but more so since my dad passed away. He was only 58 when he died. I made a pact to myself then to embrace every second, enjoy *all* experiences and never take life for granted.

This – right here, right now – isn't me. All I want is to get back to being *me*.

Yet, here I am, still sat on this floor, wanting to switch myself off from the world for a few days.

There are days when I am smashing it! Those are the days when I feel most in control and like me again. Right now though, my shit is not together ... but I won't tell anyone. Some people can see. They feel for me and say, 'I don't know how you do it!' or 'rather you than me' – those things make me feel better! I know they should probably annoy me, but they don't. I feel like people are acknowledging and validating how hard it is for me which makes it okay, somehow.

Then the silence breaks and I hear the crying. I pray I can get into that room quick enough before the other two wake up. You see, one-on-one is great, two-on-one is not so bad, but three-on-one feels impossible.

I peel myself from my spot on the kitchen floor and walk into the playroom. There he is, my beautiful, perfect, baby boy ... crying for me to hold him, settle him and feed him. I love every single inch of him. I reach into the cot to bring him close to me, to soothe him and to tell him that I'm sorry I feel like this.

His beautiful soft hand reaches up to touch me, to feel me close to him. He wants to feel safe and know that I am there for him. Every inch of my heart melts as I look into his tired, dewy blue eyes. My precious boy; *I love you so much!*

It's a miracle the other two are still asleep. I sit with my son and I breathe him in, telling him he's beautiful and holding him close to me so that he feels safe. I feed him and watch as he wriggles and squirms. Then he does it, that thing that makes the whole world stop. He locks his eyes with mine and stares at me. It's the most amazing feeling in the world. In this moment, I can breathe.

I never imagined that, when stuck in the fog, I'd feel every emotion. I suppose I always thought that people experiencing these kinds of struggles were lost and devoid of emotion. I suppose it differs for everyone but, for me, I felt every single pain, emotion, moment of anxiety and overwhelm, and every single one of them hits me hard!

Bigmouth Barbara

During the fog, Bigmouth Barbara often came into my thoughts. She was the Aldi checkout lady that broke me.

I was shopping with my little boy and noticeably pregnant with the twins. Barbara asked how far gone I was. I told her and she said, 'God, you're massive!' I should have given her the death stare and ended it right there and then. But me being me, I didn't. I explained, 'Oh, I'm having twins, that's why I'm so big!'

'Oh my God,' she said, 'Kate, this lady is having twins, look how young the one she already has is.' Everyone was staring at me. I could feel my face going crimson. My eyes were filling up. I wanted the ground to swallow me whole.

'Good luck love, you're gonna need it,' shouted Kate.

Bigmouth Barbara added: 'Not sure I would have gone through with it love, you're gonna have your hands full.'

I didn't say anything. I was mortified. How could these two strangers be so harsh to me in front of a store full of people? I packed my shopping frantically, paid and walked out.

I sat in the car and cried; I wished everyone would stop telling me how hard it was going to be.

Ok, they were right, I am *finding this hard. I wanted to prove them all wrong! But I can't because the fog won't let me.*

The problem wasn't the children or their behaviour, the problem was the fog. It was ruining everything, making me feel out of control and confused about what was going on in my life.

I appreciated that I was one of the lucky ones. I had emotional support, a network of amazing family and friends, and a husband who was a hands-on dad. He was amazing, sharing the care with me, but he still needed to work. My mum was a dream. She came, got stuck in, and helped me so much. My friends rallied around whenever they could – they knew it was hard for me.

But despite the support I had, I still felt like a failure.

I spent a lot of time looking back instead of focusing on the present moment, affecting my ability to be present with the boys, especially when the fog set in. I was frightened of losing control so I tried to control everything outside of me which only made my anxieties worse.

I was so terrified of being a failure as a mother that I didn't celebrate all the amazingly awesome things I was doing to keep the boys alive and safe every day, only seeing everything that I perceived to be wrong. I was so afraid of losing the person I was before the fog that I was missing who I had become. I spent so much time focusing on all of the things I feared that I forgot to celebrate all of the things I was doing.

It sounds simple now but it's hard to notice, let alone celebrate, the little wins when the fog takes control.

I was *always* looking back. The fog made me question *everything*.

My Why

So, why did I write this chapter? Why did I feel the need to share my vulnerability and admit that I found motherhood hard at times?

Because I want you to know that you're not alone. Parenting *is* hard at times, especially when you're battling your own mental health, and there is absolutely no shame in admitting it. I have been given an opportunity and a platform to raise awareness around motherhood and mental health. I want to shout: 'We are all in this together!'

I hope that you take some hope and reassurance that this time will pass. You are not alone, you are not a failure, you are stronger than you imagine, and whatever your struggles, you will emerge more resilient than before. If I can help just one person find the strength to get through a foggy day, then sharing my experience has been worthwhile.

Next time you feel overwhelmed and the fog starts to consume you, come back to this chapter as a little reminder to:

- Only look back to see how far you have come.

- Embrace the right here, right now (even on the toughest of days).

- Stop comparing yourself to everyone else – you do YOU!

- Notice everything you do today that keeps your family alive and safe. (I mean it – every nappy change, every feed, every cuddle, every meal made, every kiss given, etc.)

- Believe that you will come out of this stronger.

- Take every minute as it comes and don't worry about the next.

- Talk. Talk to anyone and everyone.

- Don't be afraid to tell people how you feel.

You are breakable and that's OK. And remember … you are amazing!

The fog will pass, and the sun *will* shine again.

About the Author

Laura Coote is a personal stylist and founder of online boutique Black Edge Style. In addition to being a successful entrepreneur, Laura is a proud mummy to three boys. She is a natural people-person who thrives on connecting with others, encouraging and supporting them to grow in confidence and follow their dreams. She combines her passion for supporting others with her love for style.

After working hard to overcome her own limiting beliefs and self-sabotage to create a successful business, Laura wants to empower others to overcome their fears and step into their light.

Connect With Laura:

Facebook: www.facebook.com/blackedgestyle
Instagram: www.instargram.com/blackedgestyleuk
LinkedIn: www.linkedin.com/in/laura-coote-blackedgestyle
Twitter: www.twitter.com/blackedgestyle_

When The Boat Rocks

By Nikki Bailey

'If only you could sense how important you are to the lives of those you meet; how important you can be to the people you may never even dream of. There is something of yourself that you leave at every meeting with another person.'
~ Fred Rogers

'No, I'm not a risk taker in life,' was my answer to my brother who had been talking to me about looking at a business opportunity.

Don't get me wrong, the thought of being my own boss, deciding what hours I wanted to work, and the possibility of an uncapped income stream sounded great. But, after working for Social Services for the last eighteen years, I was used to the job security and monthly payslip arriving through my door.

I loved the hands-on element of my job. Caring and supporting patients after hospital discharge often to regain their confidence and independence came with great job satisfaction and knowledge that I was making a difference. However, the politics that went on behind the scenes often drained me of joy, not to mention that my husband Mark and I were like ships passing in the night, working opposite schedules so that we could take care of our two boys.

You see, my answer was no because I was too scared to make any changes and rock the boat. Even though the hours and job didn't work for me and my overall well-being, it did work for our family needs. This is a sacrifice that many women make when they have children, isn't it? Often feeling that there isn't any other way it can be done – one of my biggest mental battles.

On the 27th of February 2014, everything changed. This was the day that something scarier came into my life, making all other internal fears pale into significance.

The Day Everything Changed

I had recently been referred to a rheumatologist due to suffering from painful flairs in my joints that had been debilitating. As part of my diagnosis and treatment plan there had been a need for lots of blood tests to be done to make sure that things were improving which, thankfully, they were. However, those blood results flagged up another issue, one that had been silently growing, possibly for some time.

On one of the earlier appointments, I vaguely remember the consultant saying the words 'blood cancer' but honestly, I hadn't taken much notice. I was sure I had misheard her. During one of our appointments, she sent me off with a blood test form which was out of the ordinary; normally the tests were done at her clinic before I went in to see her. This made me curious. So, I found myself googling the name of the test she had written on the form – yes, I am that patient that consults with 'Dr Google' but I do try to not let my mind get carried away with what I read.

The test was a very specific test to identify a protein relating to leukaemia. As I read those words, I realised that the consultant had, in fact, said 'blood cancer' at that earlier appointment – I hadn't misheard her. I felt a mixture of shock and disbelief. I mean, I was seeing her to sort out my aching joints and now I was facing the possibility that I had cancer ... It just didn't make any sense – surely, she must be wrong?

Waiting for those results to come back was one of the worst rollercoasters I have ever experienced in my life. I felt compelled to research more into the information I had found on Google, but each time I did it triggered fear inside me. I understood that the blood test was looking for a specific type of blood cancer – Chronic Lymphocytic Leukaemia (CLL) – and that it wasn't aggressive, however, it was still cancer. Cancer that was living inside my body without my knowledge.

How could this happen? was the question that kept going through my mind, along with thoughts that my consultant must be mistaken and the results would all come back clear.

So, on the morning of 27th February, I walked into my consultant's office. She smiled at me, as she always did. *It must be good news,* I thought, *she is going to say that the bloods came back clear, surely…*

'We have your results back and …' – I felt myself take a breath almost like I was preparing myself – 'it has confirmed that you do have Chronic Lymphocytic Leukaemia.' I heard her words and waited for my body and mind to react … but there was no reaction. No tears, no fear … nothing at all other than the words, 'Oh right, OK,' that came out of my mouth.

The consultant went on to say that I was CD38 negative which meant nothing to me and, for some reason, I didn't ask her what it meant. She said that this was a good marker. I told her that I had been researching CLL and that I did have some understanding of that form of cancer. I think she felt relieved; it wasn't her area of expertise. She said that I had been referred to a haematology consultant who would explain it all in more detail. Then, I left the office.

I walked back to my car, got in and broke down. It was like a delayed reaction and possibly one that I allowed myself to feel once I was alone. Having gone to the appointment alone, I now had to tell my husband, Mum, and the rest of the family that I had cancer. The thought of doing this upset me more than receiving the news myself. I knew they would be upset and scared of what it all meant and that I had to be the one to reassure them and help them to process the news. As I write this, I catch myself thinking, *how on earth did I do that when I had literally just received the news myself?* The crazy thing is that it was easier for me to be more concerned about others than it was for myself, perhaps a way of protecting me or delaying the inevitable.

After meeting my health care team at the hospital, I learnt very quickly that nothing happens fast in the world of CLL, which is both a blessing and a curse. CLL is a form of cancer that is best not to treat straight away but rather monitored in a phase known as 'Watch and Wait'. The team and I began our journey together with review appointments every three months where we watched the cancer grow a little every time. For the first few appointments I was gripped with fear and anxiety, wondering what the results would be. However, having experienced receiving the diagnosis alone, I always took someone with me to my appointments in case of bad news.

In fact, as it was my mum that attended the appointments with me, we took the opportunity to be 'ladies who lunch' after each appointment to take the focus off of it being about my cancer. Little changes in mindset grew into bigger shifts in thoughts and views which rippled out into my life in every way. This was the first time in my adult life that I had been forced to accept that this wasn't in my control. I had to learn to hand over my trust to someone I barely knew – my consultant – which meant it was important for us to build a relationship.

Taking Back Control

For me, the hardest thing at first was not knowing how the cancer was going to affect my physical ability to lead a normal life, as well as the possibility of it drastically shortening my life. After struggling with this for a little while, I decided that it was time for me to focus on the things that I *did* have control over. The things that I didn't, I was going to have to learn to let go of or live alongside.

How do you live alongside cancer? I hear you ask. Well, for me it was about making an agreement with 'Lenny'. This was the name that I gave the cancer cells that lived within my body. The agreement was that, if he behaved, I wouldn't do anything to harm him, however, once he did start misbehaving, I would serve him an eviction notice that would be enforced almost straight away. It sounds quite silly but, honestly, I really felt that I took back some power and control; I no longer needed to fear what was living inside of my body.

The next thing that I recognised to be in my control was supporting my body in its management of the cancer growing, helping it to be in its best condition to go into battle when the time came. You see, at the time I was diagnosed I was severely overweight. My body was under immense pressure to allow me to do normal day-to-day activities and I wasn't eating the most nutritious food which, in turn, meant that I struggled with my energy levels and sleep patterns.

Having tried every diet under the sun, I had only seen success using The 1:1 Diet by the Cambridge Weight Plan. So, with the agreement of the medical team, I commenced my weight loss journey. Unlike other attempts to lose weight, this time my motivation was more about my health than how I looked.

It took me three months to lose three stone. The 'eating' part was easy; the hard part was recognising poor habits and behaviours and then creating more supportive ones to make sure I went on to maintain my weight loss permanently. Each week brought another loss on the scales but, more importantly, I could feel the changes from inside my body. The aches and pains in my joints started to decrease as the pressure on them reduced and I found I was able to keep up with my two young sons when playing – something I had longed for.

Although outwardly there was a visible transformation taking place for the world to see, the biggest change was my mindset and the relationship with my body. For the first time in a long while, I felt a new level of love and respect for my body, recognising how hard it works to look after me – it never takes a break and is constantly making hard decisions on which part of me needs attention, possibly at the detriment of another part. All it ever asks of me is to listen to it, fuel it with highly nutritious food and water, move around to help strengthen the muscles, and to rest when it needs to concentrate on repairing itself. What it doesn't deserve is the harsh inner critic inside of me judging it for not looking a certain way, for it showing signs of wear and tear over the last 45 years of daily use and, in the later years, abuse.

I wish it hadn't taken a cancer diagnosis to open my eyes to just how perfectly imperfect my body was and for me to finally fall in love with it enough to show it the respect it has well and truly earnt!

As time went on, the cancer within my body grew. I started to see and feel my body struggle more and more. Even though I had the cancer, the ripple effect it caused reached out far and wide – particularly affecting my husband and my two boys. The words 'nanna nap' were heard more and more; the balance within the home changed when it came to cleaning, washing, grocery shopping, cooking, etc as my energy levels dropped lower and lower.

I started to feel like a failure as a mum, wife and human being. For years, I had been the one that supported others but now I was the one needing the support and at such a young age too.

I realised that everything I did was an exchange for my precious energy levels and with that I became more mindful of where I spent it. I needed to have more control and flexibility when it came to my work life rather than relying on a line manager needing to approve leave or time for medical appointments. However, leaving work was not an option financially.

Creating The Balance

'Have you ever thought about doing what I do?' said my weight loss consultant during one of our weekly appointments. I hadn't up until that moment, but it certainly got me thinking. *Could this be the answer to my work/life balance dilemma?* I mean, I had seen the results for myself on how well the diet and the support worked. It would also allow me to help others which has always been my purpose in life, and I would have total control over how and when I worked.

It didn't take long to think it over and, before I knew it, I had completed some training and invested in my own business. Initially, I started building my business alongside my job, until Mark (my husband) and I sat and worked out our finances and made the scary decision to hand my notice in and focus my attention and energies on building the business. The day I typed up my resignation email to my line manager and hit the 'send' button felt like a weight had been lifted off my shoulders. I knew in that moment that we had made the right decision and I can honestly say, seven years later, that I haven't had a single moment of regret.

As I write this, I am currently sat in the hospital receiving treatment as part of a clinical trial that I was very lucky to be offered, especially as the need to commence treatment started in the middle of a global pandemic. There was no need to ask for approval for leave to attend treatment appointments or worry that my income was going to be affected. My work is all done remotely thanks to changes that were made during the pandemic so I can work from anywhere at any time. I feel like I have found a perfect balance for my ever-changing energy levels. The job satisfaction I receive is immense; the personal development I have experienced has been remarkable along with the relationships I have had the honour to make.

Today, I find myself grateful for 'Lenny' coming into my life when he did. I never thought I would say that, but he really was a blessing in disguise. He brought about a personal transformation that I truly believe wouldn't have happened had he not 'arrived'.

The Nikki people meet today is a far cry from the Nikki seven years ago. I am one hundred percent comfortable in who I am. The quirks that I once hid I now embrace and understand make me unique. I am grateful for every experience I have had in life – the highs and the lows – because each one has come with a lesson that has contributed to the person I show up as every day. I understand I have touched so many lives, (as do people touch mine) and I strive to do so in a positive way. I now know what my purpose in life is; it's been there as clear as day from a young age – my heart feels full when I am in service to others.

I no longer try to change myself to fit in. I show up authentically in all my glory and with that I attract the right people into my life, letting go of those that aren't with love. I don't always get it right, but I promise to own this and learn from my mistakes. The journey of self-awareness is one that will take me to the day of my last breath on this earth and what a wonderful journey it is. To learn to love oneself unconditionally is empowering, resulting in you doing everything in your control to nurture and protect your mental and physical wellbeing.

I may once have been afraid to rock the boat and make changes in my life, but life clearly had other plans and rocked it for me! Nevertheless, through the darkest and toughest of challenges, I now find myself loving and appreciating *me*, wholeheartedly.

And that is something I never wish to change.

About the Author

Nikki Bailey (or Nikki B) is a weight loss consultant with a speciality in mindset. She celebrates the uniqueness of all the women she works with and helps them to see how perfectly imperfect they are. Nikki enables her clients to have fun rediscovering themselves throughout their transformation. She focuses on helping them to acknowledge that often food is not the problem, more so how they use that food to navigate life's challenges.

It was through her own life-changing medical diagnosis that Nikki found her passion and purpose in life, and with that she stepped into her power.

Connect with Nikki:

Facebook: www.facebook.com/one2onedietnikkib
Instagram: www.instagram.com/one2onedietnikkib
Linktree: www.linktr.ee/one2onedietnikkib

From a Flicker to a Flame

By Nicky Kilnan

Chris, you never got to finish your book, this is for you...

'I think I'll resign...'

The words came out of my mouth before I had even thought about the consequences. Before I had thought about what would come next. I wouldn't be able to go back to my previous business making bespoke candles and scents either, due to signing an employment contract which included a non-compete clause.

Those four short words were about to change everything.

It hadn't been an easy six months before that. My younger brother passing away had been a really testing period to navigate. I kept going, showing up as I always did. In fact, in true Nicky style, I was at work the following morning and carried on to keep my head out of what I was really having to face.

The universe really does like to test me.

Late December 2019

I arrived in A&E struggling like I had never struggled before. My heart felt like it was about to burst out of my chest, my breathing laboured and slow. I was finding it difficult to control my emotions as the weakness took over my body.

I glanced around the waiting room where I was waiting to be triaged. They called out number 22. I glanced down at my ticket ... number 54. There were 32 more patients to be seen before me. I didn't know how I was going to last sitting there for that long.

As the numbers started creeping up, a lady that was sitting opposite approached me. 'Here, take this,' she said. 'I'm next in, and you look like you need this more than me.' I took one look at her through my tear-filled eyes as she swapped the tickets over.

'Thank you!'

She was a kindred soul – that is exactly what I would have done if the roles had been reversed in that moment. My new number was called so I said 'thank you' again and got up to walk into the triage room. Those few steps felt like walking a mile uphill. As I sat in the chair while the nurse did my observations, I tried to calm myself. She looked at me and said, 'Wait here, I'll be back.' I thought to myself, *even if I wanted to leave, I don't think I could.*

She returned with another nurse, a doctor and a wheelchair. I was taken straight through to the majors department.

Panic set in.

'Is there anyone that can come and sit with you?' she said.

'Yes, my daughter is off today,' I said.

'Can you call her to come and sit with you?'

At that point, I hadn't told anyone I was in hospital, not even my husband, who was working overseas.

I called my daughter and husband to let them know what was happening.

Attaching me to the intravenous antibiotic drip, the medics suspected sepsis. My heart rate was through the roof and my oxygen levels were on the floor somewhere. The tests began. After what seemed like an eternity and copious amounts of poking, prodding and X-rays, the doctor came to see me. Pulling the curtain round me, he started to speak. 'We are moving you to a side room.'

At this point, I don't really remember his exact words. That 'there but not there' feeling in my ears and head made me feel like I was having an out of body experience. You know that feeling when you are beyond drunk and you can hear noises but it makes no sense? That's where I was!

He looked at me and said, ''You have influenza and pneumonia. This must have been building up for a while.'

Thinking back to how I had been feeling the last couple of weeks, working in a freezing cold environment and wearing three layers to keep myself warm, all I could think was, *thank God it's not sepsis.* The nurse returned in full PPE, wearing a mask and gloves, and handed me a face mask; I realised that I wasn't in good shape.

The next few days were spent sleeping and taking a cocktail of tablets to try and shift what I can only describe as feeling like I had been hit by a steam roller.

Christmas and New Year came and went; in fact, it may as well have been cancelled. I was struggling. I went back to the consultant who sent me for another X-ray and some lung function tests. Another course of antibiotics was handed over to me. 'There is no way you're fit enough to go back to work in that environment. I want you to have another two to three weeks off at least.'

So, I had to make the choice to return to work against consultants' orders or resign. I chose the latter. I chose to value my health, to put a value on me. Finally!

I chose to not feel unseen.

I chose to not feel undervalued.

I chose to not feel like I had done for the past few months.

So, What Next?

We were halfway through January and I had no plan. *Bugger it,* I thought, *I'm going to go out to Malaysia to gather my thoughts and try to figure out what to do next.* I called my husband. 'Book me a flight, I'm bringing munchkin over to see you.'

So, that's what he did. In three weeks' time, I would be on a plane with my youngest daughter heading out to Kuala Lumpur. Between packing and preparing for my trip I had quite a few meetings and working lunches with friends and professional colleagues. One of my clients (and now good friend) took me out for lunch one day.

'Let's do what we're good at, high-end styling for homes that are coming to the market,' she said.

We started to plan. For the first time in a long time, I felt excited. My whole being loves a polished and styled aesthetic. I had helped countless people reimagine and restyle their homes. My whole social media revolved around it; it's what I searched for, what excited me and what inspired me. Over the next few weeks, I incorporated more of that into my social media presence. It was already there, but my message needed switching up to reflect the new direction I was going in. February flew and, as I boarded the plane, I was looking forward to the sun on my face, relaxing on the beach and having massages to revive my tired body...

And the space in my head to start planning my next chapter.

Malaysia did not disappoint. The greenery was stunning and the beaches picturesque. The sea was blue, warm and idyllic. I started to get myself back into my creative groove, with all the inspiration that surrounded me; nature reignited my fire. The weekdays were spent in

Kuala Lumpur in the hustle and bustle while my husband worked. But on the weekends, that was when we travelled. I saw beauty that filled my soul with happiness. Monkeys wandered around us while we ate our breakfast on the beautiful island of Langkawi. Its Hollywood movie-style setting was breath-taking. The aquamarine sea was warm on my skin as I floated around in it. It emptied my mind of the last eight months. The white warm sand was soft on my feet as I walked along the shoreline, visioning my future. Connecting with nature in those moments of solitude brought me peace. Peace like I had not experienced in what felt like forever. We decided to go to Cherating Beach for our last trip before I was due to head home the following week. The jungle setting, built out of teak wood in the 80 acres of lush vegetation, was a completely different world. The stark contrast between this and the beautiful ocean beach just a five-minute walk away made me want to stay longer. As I sat in our cabana on the beach I blurted out, 'I want to stay longer.'

'Are you sure?' my husband said. I didn't have to think. 'Yes, I'm going to stay here for another month, I've got nothing to go home for and you get to spend more time with munchkin.'

'We can sort the flights out when we get back to Kuala Lumpur,' he said.

And that was where we left the conversation for the rest of the trip. I messaged my older children and my friends to tell them my plans. I had nothing really to rush back for. Everything I planned could be put on hold for another month. Kat, my business bestie, was glad I was enjoying the rest. She knew how the previous eight months had taken its toll on me. On more than one occasion, she would pick me up from work to find me in tears; so the fact I was relaxing and picking myself up again made her happy.

As we drove the three hours back to Kuala Lumpur, there was a lot of talk about KL going into lockdown. I didn't take much notice at the time, but little did I realise that the lockdown would be immediate and implemented the day after we returned to our apartment. We could not leave our apartment for anything – no pool, no shopping and no outdoor areas. Nothing.

All of Malaysia was in total lockdown. I hadn't taken much notice of the news when I was at home. The virus was in China. Little did we know at the time the profound impact it would have globally. For the next five days, we stayed in the apartment. Delivery drivers brought food to our apartment; breakfast was left on the tray outside. My decision was reversed – I now *wanted* to go home. Home to my older children, home to my house where I felt safe.

Navigating this next part of my journey was nothing short of terrifying. We tried to change my flights to an earlier date.

'Yes sir, we can do that for you at a charge of an extra £5000 each!' That would be £10,000 for munchkin and I to fly one-way home three days earlier than planned. We agreed I would keep the original flight. So, on the 22nd of March 2020, I started the journey back to the UK, with an asthmatic two-year-old, at the start of what was to be a worldwide pandemic. We watched the airport departure information online as flight after flight was cancelled. Kuala Lumpur to Dubai was still there!

We got into the taxi to take us to the airport. We could see the normally hectic city was like a ghost town. The airport itself was really quiet, none of the shops were open. It was functioning on the bare minimum of staff; most had left. It scared me to see how desolate a busy international airport was. Realising this situation was huge, my husband didn't want me to take the little one home, however we both felt it was for the best. The whole world was closing down around me while being stuck in the middle of Asia; it scared the living daylights out of me. Our flight stayed on the board and I managed to get to Dubai where my daughter and I faced a 24-hour wait. I booked the last room available in the airport hotel to get some sleep and to keep the little one as safe as I possibly could. Have you ever tried to entertain a two-year-old in a new environment where COVID restrictions have been implemented? She is the most sociable child I know; she will speak to anyone, and we both struggled to cope with the unfamiliar restrictions.

As we boarded the last flight from Dubai to Manchester prior to Dubai suspending all flights to the UK, the relief I felt was like nothing I'd experienced before. My Instagram followers lived the whole journey with me as I shared my snotty mess of a self the whole way home. Little did I know upon landing in the UK that we would also be in a state of lockdown. As we arrived home, I could see the panic on a lot of the travellers' faces. No one knew what was happening. I spotted my older daughter who, when she saw us, burst into tears and gave me the biggest hug I have ever known her to give. 'I never wanna go through that again,' I said. 'Just get us home.'

The next day, after a good sleep, I woke up to a million messages asking if we were home and if we were safe. We were in Day One of the UK lockdown. I was so glad to be back home with all of my children, out in the fresh air of the garden, sitting in the glorious sunshine. Yes, we had blazing sunshine on the 24th of March 2020! So, I relaxed into what I thought would be a sabbatical for a couple of weeks until this panned out. We had what felt like a staycation in the garden. We created what we christened the COVID Bar by cutting a fence panel between my house and my neighbour's -- who happened to be my aunty. We celebrated both my son and daughter's birthdays at home.

I'm not the type of person to sit and do nothing and the plan I had put in place before I went away clearly wasn't going to be happening any time soon. I spoke to a friend who then asked me to style and create her business social media aesthetics on Instagram. She saw what I had created for my businesses and my home blogging account. I said, 'Yes! I'd love to.' I mean, I wasn't gonna be doing anything else for a while so why not! And, just like that, the start of STYLESM was born.

As the next few weeks went on, my friend had so many comments about her Instagram that I could see the real benefit of this for businesses. I spoke to my business bestie and ran the idea past her. She thought this could work and wholeheartedly agreed with the concept. Just as she'd done for the previous 12 months, Kat would continue to support me, not only in business but on a personal level. And for that I will be eternally grateful.

My social media styling business was born. I quickly got my logo designed, staying true to my branding colours and keeping my look and vibe consistent so as not to confuse my audience. To my amazement, the next month saw me gain another three clients and my website was launched.

This is actually going to work, I thought to myself. My creativity, which I used for my candle making and interior styling, was beginning to be utilised to help businesses stand out in probably one of the toughest times we had seen in a long time. It felt amazing that my skill set was being noticed and appreciated to help businesses and entrepreneurs survive the pandemic. Fast forward three months and I was at full capacity with clients from around the world – the type of clients I could only dream about working with. In fact, my clients recommended me to all their friends and clients, so much so that I had a waitlist! Yes, me having a waitlist, in a business that was less than six months old!

I increased my prices and started coaching people who wanted to learn how to do it for themselves. In less than 12 months, I went from someone who had all her confidence, self-belief and tenacity boxed away to someone who had broken free and built her own empire. Taking opportunities that were presented not only got me exposure but also landed me my own television show about branding and social media on a transatlantic channel in Florida – something I could only have dreamed of before.

Even though I do not publicly show my spiritual side, many of my clients are spiritual and, I suppose, drawn to me. They have taught me so much this last year, and to those ladies I'd like to acknowledge them for their healing and support.

Lessons Learnt

What has this whole journey taught me?

That I CAN succeed, that I AM worth it. That if I AM brave enough to take that first step and believe in myself then anything is possible. My creativity is now immeasurably valued.

The pandemic forced me to prioritise myself and take time for self-care. I realised the importance of spending time with people who lift my vibrations and have great energy to be around. This whole journey has shown me that, with the right cheerleaders, true friends and self-belief, nothing can stop me.

Oh, and I forgot the most important bit…

Style … *do it with style.*

About the Author

Nicky Kilnan is a designer and stylist with a love for that luxury look. She uses her knowledge and experience to provide her clients with the best social media aesthetic whilst retaining its soul. As well as being a successful entrepreneur, Nicky is also a proud mum of four.

Forced to take her business online, Nicky quickly realised that her expertise and skills would benefit Instagram business accounts. Within a very short time, she has become the go-to girl globally for getting a polished and scroll-stopping grid look. She has combined her love of style with helping people raise their social media game and express their true authentic selves.

Connect With Nicky:

Website: www.stylesm.com

Facebook: www.facebook.com/stylesm

Instagram: www.Instagram.com/stylemy_sm

Living Life on My Terms

By Alison Dee

'Nothing is impossible. The word itself says I'm possible.'
~ Audrey Hepburn

It was a cold and stormy February evening. Water poured through the leak in the roof. A fan heater provided the only warmth (the heating had broken … again). Sat on a dilapidated sofa with my beloved cat Gizmo, I wondered what I was doing with my life.

Fresh out of an abusive relationship and back in the house that I thought I would never return to, I'd hit rock bottom.

I was in £18.5k of credit card debt and feeling suffocated by my situation. My not-so-nice ex had alienated almost everyone from my life, including making the relationship with my parents incredibly strained. I felt so lost and alone.

I didn't like the person I'd become at all; I wasn't happy with myself in so many ways. I knew I was capable of so much more but was stuck in a minimum wage, temporary, basic admin job. Where had that shiny, high-flying career gone, with a company car, laptop and endless lunches out? How had it come to this?

I was overweight, the heaviest I'd ever been – I felt so uncomfortable in my own skin. I was crippled with depression and anxiety. I felt a total mess and my inner turmoil was reflected in the disaster of my life.

That cold and stormy February evening was the turning point in my life. I swore that if I ever found my way out of the situation I was in, I would devote myself to helping others so that no one would ever have to feel as lost as I did. I didn't know how that would look, or if it was even possible. It seemed a laughable goal that anyone could be inspired by little old me, or that I would even have the capacity to help anyone, but I knew things needed to change for my own sanity. And I realised in that moment, an epiphany if you will, that only I could make that change. How? I had no idea. But it was up to me and me alone.

My 'Kick-Me' Sign

I'd never been happy with myself. I was lost in people-pleasing and got taken advantage of too many times by people I thought were friends. I was desperate to be around people – *any* people. I felt I was wearing a sign on my back saying 'kick me'. I got swept along by life, always doing what others thought I 'should' do. It wasn't fun. I had awful social anxiety, forever worrying what others would think of me and if I fitted in. I hated being alone because that's when the intrusive thoughts would take over.

So, I made it my mission to rarely be alone, not realising that no one else was responsible for that feeling of loneliness inside of me. The busier I was, the lonelier I felt, but because I was so busy I had no time to dwell on it or work out how to change it.

That February evening was the turning point. I decided that I had to choose. Life *could* be different … if only I knew *how*?

I started developing a positive mindset. Yes, I wanted to be in a loving relationship, but I also recognised I needed time to heal and that I couldn't fully control when I was going to meet someone. I also promised myself that I'd rather stay single than be in another relationship feeling alone – being ignored by your partner while in the same room is the loneliest feeling of all. I promised myself that when I met someone they would complement my life, but I wouldn't need them to complete it because it would already be full and complete.

So, I decided to focus on three things I *could* control: getting my finances in order (and finding a better job), losing weight, and getting my social life back on track. I threw myself into old habits and what I knew, becoming so busy that I didn't have to think about what was going on inside me.

I got a new job that seemed to have prospects *and* it was closer to home. I revived my social life in the most incredible way and lost a lot of weight. I even met a wonderful man and we began our relationship. Then I got the opportunity to finally build a career and qualify as a biomedical scientist. Everything I'd longed for was happening – to be living happily with my partner in my house, with my cat Gizmo and a career I could be proud of.

Everything was coming together and I was finally living my dream…

But still, I wasn't happy.

I was still chasing something I couldn't identify. I still didn't like me or my own company, and I started to realise that nothing external could bring me what I didn't feel within. I'd never particularly liked myself to begin with but my ex had made all of my insecurities so raw. I'd second-guess myself on absolutely everything. Outwardly, everything looked great; I exuded confidence. On the inside, I was crippled with low self-confidence and constant anxiety.

Somehow, I started to realise that true inner peace and happiness had to come from me. The job and how everything looked from the outside was merely a sticking plaster masking the real problems underneath. As a child, I'd developed people-pleasing tendencies. I wasn't aware of what I wanted or what would make me happy. How do you even begin to work out what you want when you've lived your whole life for others' wants and needs?

The Turning Point

In my mid-thirties, I was beginning to feel as lost and alone as I did back on that cold, stormy February evening. I had everything I thought I'd ever wanted – the amazing social life, loving partner and 'prestigious' career – and yet I still didn't know who 'Alison' was. I had made so much progress only for it to all come crashing back down.

I got screwed over by a set of friends – old patterns were still re-emerging and I felt powerless to stop them. Powerless to be in control of my life yet again. It felt as though my life was running me, not the other way around.

I felt utterly physically and mentally exhausted with life in general … and then I got diagnosed with chronic fatigue syndrome. I spent two months in bed, unable to function.

I hadn't hit rock bottom this time but it felt like another level of rock bottom – feeling just as helpless, albeit in entirely different circumstances.

I'd tried the 'sticking plaster' approach by making my life look good from the outside but it clearly wasn't working, otherwise I wouldn't be bed-bound. I didn't even have the energy to think. I was thoroughly exhausted and sick of life – I didn't have anything left in me to give.

I was stuck yet again.

And then I came across a lady who introduced me to the *Miracle Morning* by Hal Elrod. It introduced me to the concept of mindset work – something, I realised, that I had been unconsciously doing already (to a point). Now, I'm not a morning person – never have been and I don't ever plan to be – but I took on board what Hal was saying about developing your mindset daily.

I'd never thought about something like working on your mind as being the key to changing your life. I'd always thought it came from external things. It all sounded rather 'woo-woo' to me.

But it also sounded like such a simple concept. I started doing affirmations daily, saying them under my breath as I walked from my car into the hospital where I worked, feeling utterly daft. I mean, how could these positive statements change how I think?

I also learned about having a daily gratitude practice and started finding gratitude for the small things in my life. This definitely didn't come easily to me, what with being a glass-half-empty person, but I persevered.

Well, as it turns out, it does work. I *did* start feeling better about myself. I felt more confident. I started talking about what I wanted to do with my life and I began dreaming again, something I don't remember doing since I was a child.

I started to flip how I was thinking. Instead of dwelling on the *negatives* (and oh boy, did I love to dwell on the negatives), I started seeing *positives* or lessons. I started detaching myself from situations and not internalising things as much.

I used to be so incredibly sensitive that I'd take offence at the drop of a hat, all because of how I felt inside. I started being calmer and began to gain acceptance of myself.

I decided to start living life for *me*. I didn't know how that looked yet. I just knew that I'd spent my whole life doing what others thought I should do. I was still in debt, still unable to do what I wanted, when I wanted, and I wanted that to change.

It was hard to step forward and say I was going to break away from the crowd; away from the expectations that had been placed on me all my life. I really had to start upping my mindset game and figuring out exactly how and why what I was doing wasn't working.

Being swept along with the crowd and societal expectations for so long meant I had little to no boundaries. I'd say yes out of guilt even though I desperately wanted to say no. If I had a free evening I wouldn't stick to the plans I'd made with myself when someone asked me to make plans with them. I'd made a rod for my own back with how busy I'd become and it was a whole new level of exhaustion.

So, I learnt what boundaries were – that saying no was possible. It didn't mean you were a bad person (the people-pleaser in me took a long time to register that) and I started learning I could make *me* a priority.

How's that for a game changer?!

Did you notice back on that stormy February evening that not one of the three goals I set for myself was for me or to be happy? They were all about external things. All about how I thought it would look to others; it was all about the image I was projecting.

Well, I decided to set a new goal – to love myself and be happy and content with *me* and *my* life. And if I wasn't, I needed to work out what I had to change in order to get to that place.

I threw myself into mindset work – not just doing it but understanding how the mind worked. I became obsessed with personal development books, amassing a rather impressive personal library and eagerly devouring any knowledge I could. I signed up to free challenge after free challenge, eventually deciding to invest in myself and hire a coach. (The first one was a disaster but I've found better ones since then!)

I learnt how to make me a priority and that self-care isn't just about nice bubble baths (although I do love a good bubble bath with candles and wine). It's about boundaries, the priorities in your life (with you at the top), and ultimately following the path that makes you happy.

I finally found my tribe – *my* people – who understand me as a soul. I learnt how to protect my energy around those who don't have good intentions and how to spot them. I think that was the biggest learning curve of my life.

I started helping others – as I vowed I would.

People do tell me I'm inspiring now. I find that so humbling. Through all the trials and tribulations, I finally found my passion and purpose and it's not in a million years how I dreamed it would look.

I've always been a very loving and giving person and that was never a bad thing. It was learning to channel it in the right way that I needed to figure out.

And all of this was about me, not the people around me - they can't give to me what I don't give to myself. I learnt to love, respect and honour myself for who I am. And that's what changed *everything*.

I've learnt that life is an ever-evolving, never-ending journey of self-development. There are always new things to learn and new lessons to implement; we become better people the more we pursue our own self-development. If we aren't happy within, we can't give to others and help to enhance their lives. There's a reason they tell you on aircrafts to fit your own oxygen mask first – you have to help yourself before helping others. You have to learn that *you* are in control of your life.

The only person who can ever truly change your life is *you*. You have the power within – is it time for you to recognise your power, step forward and start creating the life you have dreamed of? It's not a smooth, plain sailing journey at all but I can assure you, from my journey, that through all the twists and turns and ups and downs, it is most definitely worth it.

This is a journey you don't have to take all on your own. My stubbornness wouldn't allow me to be vulnerable and admit I didn't have it all figured out. I learnt I could reach out, that I could learn from others, and that doing so didn't make me any less of a person. In fact, all this new knowledge meant I could show up and share the message even wider.

I'll never forget that lost, upset, tired girl on that stormy February evening. She's part of me and my story. I wish I could reach back and give her a cuddle and tell her that everything will turn out okay. Everything I'm doing now would have surpassed her wildest dreams…

And I'm only just getting started.

About the Author

Alison Dee is a certified life coach, mindset mentor & NLP practitioner. After discovering *The Secret* in 2011, and learning how powerful the mind is, she shifted her mindset in 2014 following the end of a mentally abusive relationship. Alison is now a qualified biomedical scientist and an expert in positive mindset, manifestation and attraction marketing. She integrates science and spirituality to make creating your dream life understandable and accessible – even to the greatest cynics!

In 2020, Alison founded the Positive Mindset Tribe – a supportive community to learn, grow and celebrate your life's milestones. Addicted to crystals and personal development books, Alison is happiest when hanging out with her wonderful partner Jason and her cats – preferably with a glass of wine!

Connect With Alison:

Website: www.dee-lightfulliving.com
Facebook: www.facebook.com/alison.d.clarkson
Instagram: www.instagram.com/i_am_alisondee

Was I Worthless as a Woman?

By Lisa Williams

We all have the ability to be enough, no matter your pain you can achieve your desires.

I lay transfixed on the hard, narrow hospital bed, my eyes closed, hoping that my dream would become reality. The room was dark and still. A long empty silence filled the room; it seemed like a lifetime before any words were spoken. The words which followed were distant but gentle. All I could think was, *why me?*

As a child, I craved a loving family unit. My mum was a single parent and my relationship with my father began at nine years old. It was a very robotic relationship with no emotional connection. I never had that warm fuzzy feeling. I never had hugs that made me feel safe. I certainly never felt loved by him. When I fell pregnant with Alysa at age 26, I was thrilled. I could not wait to be a mum. I had an exceptionally smooth pregnancy with no complications. She was born in April 2013 with a full head of jet-black hair. I remember the midwife saying, 'I bet you had terrible heartburn.' I could not wait to share my joy with the world. When I became a single mum a year later, I was deflated. I felt like I had failed. This was not the dream I had envisioned. There were times when Alysa tested me by throwing her food and mimicking my lack of eating. I often felt like I had failed as a mother. My heart had been tested on several occasions, but I dug deep and found the strength to move forward and be the best mum I could.

Alysa was a funny character. Her speech was fantastic for her age, and she would often burst out into song, typically *Let It Go* from the *Frozen* soundtrack. I loved watching her sing and dance with her long blonde hair and piercing blue eyes. It made me feel exhilarated. Alysa was just 18 months old when I met Phil. Phil was kind and caring with a warm heart and a kind smile which made his brown eyes sparkle. He was everything I had always desired in a man, a complete contrast to any man that had been a part of my life before. Phil opened his arms and welcomed us both into his heart. Alysa and Phil developed a bond like two naughty school kids, laughing at the same jokes and giggling at silly YouTube videos. As I watched their bond grow, I knew that this was what family was meant to be like. I would often sit and watch Alysa and Phil play and wonder what life would be like if we had our own child. Who would they look like? Would they have blonde or brown hair? Would they have brown or hazel eyes? I would be awash with elation thinking about extending our family. This desire grew stronger over the years.

My Heart Broke

In July 2016, it was my cousin's wedding. I wore a beautiful white A-line dress with large pink, purple and blue flowers. Phil wore a slim-fit, navy-blue suit with a light blue shirt. I would say we looked the perfect couple. I felt amazing! I had my hair and makeup done and my dream man on my arm – what more could I need? I woke up the next morning in so much pain. I did not even have the energy to go and collect my car from the church yard. I curled up on the sofa next to Phil. I had never experienced anything like this. I stood up and a gush of blood poured from me. The pain in my lower abdomen was excruciating, my knees felt weak, my body was sweaty. I slowly walked towards the bathroom, grabbing hold of the walls as I pulled my heavy, weak body upstairs. As I pulled my pyjama bottoms down slowly, unsure what to expect, I saw blood. Inside the masses of bright red blood was a large clot. This clot was my baby. Feeling numb, not understanding what had happened, my mind raced with questions. I quickly cleaned myself up and flushed everything away. I went back downstairs, distant and cold; my body was there but my head was not.

Over the next few days, I knew something wasn't right. I was tired, weak, and extremely low, so I took myself to the doctors where they confirmed I was pregnant. Until this point, I had kept these thoughts and feelings to myself. I didn't even tell Phil what had happened that day in the bathroom. I was referred to the EPU (Early Pregnancy Unit). Sitting in the waiting room you could hear a pin drop. A dull, intense silence addled with nerves and anxiety filled the room – it was torture. I began to sweat. My name was called. Heart pounding, I entered the dark room. Laying my weak, tired body on the examination bed, I was informed that I had miscarried. I felt numb. I later found out I was around eight weeks pregnant. As this news began to sink into my weakened body, I was devastated. I felt broken, torn apart. Having lost my future husband's child, I began to self-sabotage, telling myself I was 'worthless as a woman'. I began to hate my body. I hated myself for not being able to carry a baby. I hated myself for not knowing I was pregnant. I hated myself for being overweight. I hated every inch of my skin, slowly slipping into comfort eating. I did not know how to talk to anyone so I kept these thoughts inside my head. I was fighting my inner demons over loss, grief, and self-worth.

The next few months went by in a blur; I lived my life on autopilot. Work, home, and sleep. The negative self-talk continued to occupy my days. At that time, I was working for an estate agent in the accounts department. I had a large office to myself on the third floor of an old, dated building which was cold; the windows whistled in the wind.

One cold winter's day in January, I felt tired, exhausted and my head was pounding. I struggled to make it to the third floor. I was physically drained. Deep down I knew something was not right. I took myself home, the 30-minute journey feeling like a lifetime. I gazed out at the fields while driving, my mind buzzing. I remember thinking, *could I be pregnant?* Instantly I brushed the thought away but it re-emerged. I stopped at the local Sainsbury's to get a test. At this moment in my life, the ten pound pregnancy test was way over my budget so I talked myself out of buying one. I remember thinking, *no you can't be, go home to bed.* As I dragged my tired body out of the store I opened the car door, climbed in slowly and drove home, bewildered. I crawled slowly into bed, shut the curtains, and tried to block the voices out of my head. During this period, I never actively did any self-care. I was also a people-pleaser and often put others first. On this day, I was due to go to a friend's 30th birthday party. So, true to my nature, I put on my black floating dress, got in my car (with Phil sat beside me), and off we went on the 40-minute journey. It was a dull winter's drive; the roads were quiet after the busy festive period. The drive was impassive, although I felt slightly better in myself that the journey lacked emotion. Thoughts of being pregnant remained in my head.

We arrived at the party; it was bustling. I mingled with my group of university friends, chatting about old times and current lives. The energy was fantastic but I seemed to be annihilating myself. A wave of panic washed over me as I gripped my stomach as the first pain swiped. Composing myself I walked towards the bathroom. My black knickers were sopping with bright red blood. I quickly filled my tights and knickers with as much tissue as possible, left the bathroom, found Phil and demanded, 'We need to go. NOW!' I quickly said my goodbyes, apologised for leaving early and left. Outside I told Phil what had happened. His face dropped. I will never forget that glazed look on his face. Shivering from the cold I placed an old plastic bag to protect the car seat, crying with every cramping pain that swept over me. We drove straight to A&E.

By the time I got to the hospital I could barely stand; I was crippled with pain. I remember sitting in the waiting area and knowing this feeling was the same. I was checked over, told to rest and return on Monday for a scan. That weekend was torture – knowing you are miscarrying and having those same feelings, the blood, the pain and undesirable thoughts in your head.

On Monday, each step echoed as I walked along the empty hospital corridors. The knot inside my stomach was so tight; I felt sick as I gave my name to the gentleman at the desk. As we took our seats in that same room, with that same dull silence, my heart raced. The room had the same layout, the same nurses, the same numb look on the patients' faces. Inside the dark black room, those same words: 'I am afraid there is nothing in your womb.' I lay motionless as tears filled my eyes and Phil's hand gripping mine a little tighter. My body had failed me again.

Getting Out of the Rut

I felt so low, I had never been in such a dark place! I knew something had to change. I could not carry on using food as my security blanket, I couldn't stay in that dark rut. I remember waking up and wanting it to be bedtime. I felt so lethargic and despondent each day. I would look in the mirror and physically recoil at my reflection – I loathed my worthless body. I needed to learn to love *me*.

I remember sitting in my office on a cold winter's day, physically and emotionally alone. I was in my head of hatred, feeling low and empty, completely isolated with nowhere to go and no one to turn to. I had to get out of this psychological mess I was in. As I sat in my office chair a bold, courageous woman lit up my phone. Her fearless, confident spirit made me aspire to have her confidence. Without hesitation I clutched my phone and signed up to her company. The company's mission was to uplift, empower and validate. In that moment, I was aspiring to be confident. I didn't care about the practicalities – I just wanted to feel loved and love me again. I had zero idea what it entailed; I would have tried anything to get out of the dark hole which was consuming my life. Something in that instant guided me to that opportunity. Only now, looking back, do I realise that it was my awakening; it was a pivotal moment in my life.

As part of my journey I was required to take selfies. At first, I hated it. I would cringe looking at them and it would take several attempts before one was good enough. During this time, I was introduced to self-development. I had never done anything like this before, it was all new to me. I remember the first ever book I read about unlocking the secrets to success, sanity, and happiness. I used to listen to this while I drove to work; it made a huge impact on me and my day. Then one day it all clicked, I began to live my life in line with the universe. I finally believed in myself. My confidence was growing. I even began doing live videos which was a huge leap from detesting my selfies. I absolutely loved my time in network marketing during those three years; the skills I learned were paramount to my future life. I will be forever grateful for the confidence that the journey cultivated within me. The love I once craved became the love I lead my everyday life with. Mindset is something I make part of my daily routine; it is a vital element to living life on your terms. I even gave up my job in that big, huge office that filled me with painful memories of loss. I trusted that the universe had a plan ... and it did.

March 2018, I shared my first public post about my miscarriage journey stating how I was 'one-in-four women'. My post was flooded with comments about how brave and inspirational I was. So many people shared their own stories about miscarriage which made me realise I was not alone and this subject was still very taboo. This was the day my healing began. I used my pain and turned it into my passion – my passion for extending my family, my passion for my business, my passion to move forward. In June 2018, I created my first ever vision board and booked our local positivity coach for a group session at my house. One of my earliest manifestations was getting a picture with Gary Barlow, an idol of mine. I had learned all the mindset tools in books over the years which I implemented within the board. I quickly became infatuated with my board and vision boards in general. The power of a board fascinated me and still does. This led me to the next stage of my journey – becoming a vision board facilitator. I remember sitting on the vision board course having so many buzzing ideas of how this would develop into something amazing. It lit a fire inside me.

A Better Place

My personal life was going amazing, I had a job I enjoyed, and confidence in myself and my abilities. Alysa was doing fantastic at school and had taken up a keen interest in horse riding. I was also promoted from 'girlfriend' to 'fiancée'. November 15th, 2018, I stood at the top of the stairs. 'Phil,' I shouted, my hands shaking, staring at the two lines on the test tube in my hand. Phil ran to me, unsure what was happening. He was lost for words. This was our time; the universe had listened. I began visualising life with the baby. All my dreams were finally coming true. I spent lots of time resting; I didn't do anything to jeopardise the baby. I knew getting through the next few weeks was the hardest part. Each time I went to the toilet, fear would cripple me; each time I felt a twinge, I would stop still in silence. Two weeks went by and I found myself in that familiar dark room. I had some bleeding but no pain. So, I held my faith in the universe and while lying on the hard narrow hospital bed with my eyes firmly shut, I longed for a voice to say, 'We have a heartbeat.' Those words never came. There was no heartbeat. Just silence. During the next three months, the anguish remained. While my body didn't experience any physical pain from this loss, the emotional pain was excruciating. I had to go back to that same hospital, daily, weekly, then fortnightly for three months as the hormones from the baby did not want to leave my body. Each visit was a reminder of loss, of failure … a kick in the stomach. My heart was broken. I had lost my faith in the universe and I found myself back in that dark rut of *why me?*

This time I didn't wallow. I needed to understand my feelings. So, I turned to self-development, looking for books on how to live after your child dies. I needed to understand my emotional vibrations. These were my babies, they were a part of me, they were who formed me into the person I am today. I asked Phil if he would mind us holding a ceremony and naming our children. Of course, Phil was as supportive as ever and agreed. I wanted our babies to feel part of us. During this time of gaining clarity on the loss and planning a ceremony, I had an enlightened idea that we should get married at the same ceremony! I felt like I could breathe again, I felt clear, I had a new direction to focus on.

We booked our wedding and naming ceremony for 15th November 2019, one year to the day that we held that last pregnancy test. This date seemed perfect for us, not only to celebrate our wedding but also to honour our unborn children. I walked up the aisle to Rachel Platten's *Better Place;* my world had become a better place since Phil had come along. We stood side by side at the altar. The church was cold, I was clammy, my heart was beating quickly. Phil looked anxious as the vicar softly spoke our babies' names – Joy, River and Rain. Tears ran down my face. I could feel the emotion in the church, I could feel the pain. As my tears fell and we both said, 'I do', I felt the colours of the rainbow shine inside me.

I've since welcomed my beautiful rainbow daughter Talia into the world, completing our family. I'm living the dream, standing proud as the 'Vision Board Queen', and helping others do the same. Life may have thrown many curveballs and a huge dose of heartache my way, but now I know, wholeheartedly, that I *am* worthy of love, happiness and success ... and so much more.

About the Author

Lisa Williams, aka the 'Vision Board Queen', is a trained vision board facilitator who works with businesswomen to create the blueprints for their dream life. Through vision boarding, Lisa has achieved several of her visionary dreams, including her dream wedding and rainbow baby.

Lisa is extremely passionate about vision boards and the law of attraction, running sell-out online courses to help people to achieve their dreams. Lisa is also a well-known online speaker in the vision board field. She enjoys helping and supporting businesswomen to learn, grow and connect as a networking leader.

Lisa believes that having consistency and setting goals is the key to achieving your dreams. Her mission is to leave a legacy for her girls.

Connect With Lisa:

Website: www.lisawilliams-lmg.co.uk/vision-board-workshops
Facebook: www.facebook.com/groups/visionboardqueen

From Analytical Cynic to 'Weird Witchy Woman' - and Proud of It!

By Karolyn McPherson

'The wings of transformation are born of patience and struggle.' ~ Janet S Dickens

During my Reiki attunement, Roberta said, 'Your necklace has become so hot because your dragon's energy is being released.' My inner voice said, *what on earth are you talking about? Why would you mention dragons?* However, there was no denying that I felt the heat and something shifting in my chest. Was it the energy? I remembered that I was born in the Chinese year of the dragon and, from childhood, I'd often dreamt of dragons. *How could Roberta possibly have known that? Was it a coincidence that she'd mentioned dragons in particular?* Somehow, I knew it wasn't. I felt lighter, a sense of release and elation. Maybe the unfurling of the dragon

wings was symbolic of opening the connection to universal energies, reinforcing my inner strength? This realisation was the spark that ignited my spiritual journey.

Character Building in Progress

I'd always been pretty level-headed. Analytical (some might say cynical) of spiritualists and 'weird witchy things', I was one of those inquisitive children always asking, 'But why?' My job as an NHS radiographer (and now sonographer) is science based, requiring knowledge and understanding of physics and analytical skills. Now I believe that my chosen career as a sonographer working with the energy of piezo electric crystals wasn't simply by chance.

From childhood, I was drawn to rocks and crystals. My dad encouraged me to collect and carry pebbles in my pockets, while my grandma and Mum indulged me with crystal jewellery. Growing up, I'd choose my jewellery first before deciding on the outfit to fit around it. It wasn't until I was older that I became aware that instinctively I'd been drawn to specific crystals on different days because they were what I needed energetically.

During my sonography clinical training, I didn't feel valued or supported. The NHS was run in a hierarchical and patriarchal manner. I was given little encouragement from my trainer. It was a challenging and stressful experience; I seriously considered giving up and changing my career.

I was regularly referred to as 'the wee lassie', shouted at and put down in front of patients. For example, one of the consultants would supervise me performing an examination, often saying, 'Rubbish, don't even bother taking that image. For goodness sake, can't you see that?' I wasn't given any explanation of how to improve things or where I'd gone wrong.

I was subjected to temper tantrums. On one occasion, a consultant went ballistic, ranting about what a 'disgusting state' I'd left the ultrasound probe in, adding that he'd hate to see what my house looked like if that was my standard of cleanliness! He was almost purple with rage when I dared to interrupt him to explain that I hadn't used the equipment and that it was, in fact, one of his consultant colleagues.

On another occasion, a doctor threw a book at me because I wasn't fast enough cutting corners or manipulating the results in the way that he wanted me to. On complaining and reporting the incident to my manager, I was told, 'He's a consultant, you're just a trainee. Deal with it!' To my knowledge, there wasn't an anti bullying policy at that time. If there was, it certainly wasn't highlighted.

Despite the lack of support, I found the courage and inner strength to continue and didn't compromise on anything that I felt to be professionally and morally wrong. However, that didn't make things easy or gain me popularity with a few of my senior colleagues.

The most difficult and distressing part of the job was discovering problems during pregnancy scans and having the awful responsibility of giving world-shattering, heart-breaking news to expectant mothers and their partners. It was an emotionally charged rollercoaster. I struggled dealing with the array of emotions I'd feel from the distraught couples, ranging from anger, disbelief, denial and desolation, along with my own feelings of deep sadness, fear of making a mistake or misdiagnosis, and guilt for being the one delivering the devastating news. One day early on, when I was particularly upset and physically shaking, I overheard my trainer say within earshot, 'She's just not got broad enough shoulders like me.'

Retrospectively, I realise my trainer felt threatened as she didn't have the qualification that I went on to have. She was trying to assert herself by putting me down and saw me as competition so wanted to keep her knowledge to herself. I was young, compassionate, sensitive, keen to learn, enthusiastic, and wanted to do my best for the patients with their examinations and in treating them as sensitively as possible. However, the harder I tried to improve, thinking that it would please her, the more threatened she seemed.

Rather than feeling embittered about my experience, the lesson taught me to be a better, more patient, empathetic sonographer and mentor.

Although I didn't feel it at the time, I am grateful to these teachers. I vowed that I wouldn't treat anyone the way I was treated. I wouldn't want anyone to feel the way I did. Throughout my career in the NHS, working in different hospitals in varying positions, my role as a mentor has always been something that I really enjoy. Sharing knowledge, working together, helping people develop their skills, watching them grow and recognising their strengths is something that brings me joy rather than feeling threatened or seeing it as something that diminishes my standing.

Champion Cheerleader

My self-confidence was close to rock bottom. I was mentally and physically exhausted, I suffered insomnia and was irritable and short-tempered, particularly with my husband (isn't it always the ones closest to us that are affected the most). It put a huge strain on my marriage. (I am so grateful and fortunate that he is so easy-going, patient and supportive; he's always been my cheerleader.) I frequently felt nauseous at the thought of going to work and suffered painful irritable bowel symptoms. My parents use the expression 'character building' when experiencing setbacks and challenges. This experience was definitely 'character building' and shaped the person I am today.

I knew I needed to do something to help deal with the stress but, at the time, mental health issues were still taboo subjects. I didn't want to be labelled as I believed it would jeopardise my career, especially in view of the environment I was working in. So, I looked for alternatives which is how I came upon Reiki. This was at a time when acupuncture wasn't given any credence in the NHS and Reiki was considered complete 'mumbo jumbo'. Therefore, not surprisingly, I didn't mention my Reiki experience at work because I was afraid of judgement and ridicule. I couldn't explain or understand how it worked myself and was still trying to get my head around it too.

Practicing Reiki didn't mean that everything was miraculously rosy. The Reiki principles, which are pretty much the basis of what's now known as mindfulness, helped me to learn to relax more, develop better coping strategies, be kinder to myself and less self-critical. While I still felt compassion and empathy, I no longer took on the emotional burden of others or felt responsible for their behaviours.

With the huge support and patience of my husband, whilst also being proactive in my self-care and strengthening my resolve and determination to 'not let them beat me', I passed all the exams and clinical assessments to qualify in ultrasound. Shortly after, I was promoted to a senior position. However, the experience left me striving to prove myself and suffering from self-doubt and lack of confidence for many years.

As Reiki began to become more important in my life I discussed and practised healing on my close friends and family, despite some ridicule. I was intrigued and bewildered by the effects I'd experienced for myself. Although I didn't fully trust my instincts yet and wasn't totally convinced about the healing effects for others, I found that the more I practised, the more I was able to sense where the flow of energy was needed.

The turning point – when I became more confident in trusting my abilities to channel energy and convinced about the beneficial healing effects on others – was on a skiing holiday.

Doubting Duo Bewitched?

We were with a group of friends, one of whom was a burly 6'3″ straight-talking Glaswegian with a gruff, gravelly voice from a throat that had smoked a thousand cigarettes. With his broad accent and rapid speech I struggled to understand most of what he said except the expletives which peppered every sentence. He was a rough diamond, brutally honest yet kind at heart – swearing was part and parcel of his normal conversation.

One afternoon, when on a chairlift together, I felt the energy beginning to flow through my hands. When I noticed him rubbing his knee I realised it was meant for him so I offered to do some Reiki. His response was, 'WTF is reckty?' Then, after laughing raucously, he said,

'Aww, awright batter oan wee man,' which translates as, 'OK, go ahead little person.'

I explained that I could feel the energy going to specific areas where it was needed and that it was clearing blockages to the energy flow. He said he felt heat and 'weird tingling', joking that it was my magic touch and I'd always made him feel weak at the knees! (ha, ha!) Later that evening, when preparing to head out for dinner, there was a knock at the door. To my surprise, it was my Glaswegian friend, sheepishly asking if I'd do some more of that 'reckty stuff' because it felt better and he'd not had to take more painkillers. I was delighted for him and felt elated at the results.

Confirmation that I'd finally let go of the fear of judgement from others came weeks later at work. I was working with a consultant, regarded by colleagues to be intolerant and intimidating but who I found to be dedicated to his patients. He had high standards and was someone I had great respect for. I noticed his awkward body position and, without thinking, automatically adjusted the table height for him. Silence descended. All eyes turned on me. I pointed out that it was a better position for him and that what he was doing could cause him neck pain. He admitted that he was suffering neck pain. Instinctively without thinking I offered to do some Reiki, his response being, 'I don't believe in that weird stuff.' Without hesitation, I answered that I believed in it and felt it would work regardless of whether he believed it or not.

The consultant was surprised that I could accurately pinpoint the painful areas, justifying it by saying he must've told me. The following day, he sought me out to say he'd felt better but thought it was just a coincidence rather than the Reiki. Nevertheless, he wanted to try again for 'experimental purposes'. When he returned a third time he conceded that it was making a difference, calling me a 'weird witchy woman'. My response: 'Yes, I am! And I'm going to start charging you for my services!'

Dragon Wings Unfurled

My trust in my intuition and what I believe is spiritual guidance continues to become stronger as I have let go of all fear of judgement. Another example of this is in relation to crystals. I was going to visit someone who had been a previous work colleague. Despite not working closely together or knowing each other well, we'd kept in touch occasionally over the years by text. She'd contacted me to ask me to share some advertising leaflets for her new business, coinciding with me deciding to branch out and launch my own business. So, we arranged to meet up for lunch and discuss the possibility of supporting each other. Directly before leaving to head out I had an overwhelming urge to take two crystals with me; intuitively I knew they were for her. My past self would have ignored the feeling, gone without them and made no mention of it, not wanting to appear or be thought of as strange.

On meeting her, the feeling that the crystals were for her intensified and I had a strong sense that she needed Reiki too. I didn't want to unsettle her by leading with this straight away so asked if she was OK. She said she wasn't feeling 100 percent but didn't elaborate. During lunch, while telling me about her exciting new venture and business plans, I could feel the energy building. I asked if she'd allow me to give her some Reiki which might help her feel better and that I had some crystals for her if she'd like them. She said, 'You're weirding me out a bit but OK, I trust you.' I gave her the crystals to hold in each hand, one of which was a citrine.

She said, 'Funny, I've been thinking about buying this as a piece of jewellery.' Confirmation that it was indeed meant for her. Immediately, powerful energy began flowing to her left side around her kidney area and towards her bladder. As she was a nurse I said, 'We both know this is around your kidney area. This isn't diagnosing anything; it just means for whatever reason that energy is needed in this area.' She said she felt her side warming up and admitted that she had been running to the toilet all day and thought she probably had a urine infection. (Citrine is a crystal said to be good for bladder and kidney infections – no coincidence, it was meant for her.)

I hadn't felt such a strong concentration of energy flowing before, so I suggested it was worth getting a urine sample done and not leaving things too long which she said she would. A few days later, I got a message thanking me for the crystals, the Reiki, and for encouraging her to seek help as she probably wouldn't have gone as quickly to have her symptoms checked out. It was an infection with blood in the urine and, on further investigation, it was discovered that she had a kidney stone in her left kidney which required hospital admission for treatment. Hers was one of the first Facebook reviews when I launched my holistic business, saying that she was 'freaked out' by my ability to pinpoint the problem area and how grateful she was that I had encouraged her to seek help. She thought I was a weird witchy woman. I'm happy to agree with that statement because it is part of who I am!

The word 'weird' originally meant destiny or fate which I believe for me is practicing energy healing, working with crystals and sharing these gifts and knowledge. I don't feel offended being called weird; on the contrary it feels empowering to show this aspect of my true self. I no longer fear the judgement or opinion of others, or the way they perceive me. Accepting and understanding that none of these things are my responsibility is liberating.

I finally feel comfortable with who I am, confident and able to trust my intuition, centre myself, feel from my heart, and listen less to my analytical brain telling me to keep quiet in relation to healing and spiritual matters. I recognise and accept that this intuitive aspect of me enhances rather than hinders, and makes me whole, bringing balance to my analytical side.

My inner dragon has been released and is ready to soar!

About the Author

Karolyn McPherson is an intuitive healer, Reiki Master teacher and guardian of crystal dragons. She has worked with the magical power of crystals to transform one form of energy into another, allowing physical ailments to be seen within the body.

Working in her role as a sonographer, dealing with others' ailments, stresses and anxieties has allowed Karolyn to develop and hone her communication and intuitive skills. Karolyn's unconventional skills have enabled her to quickly identify and focus on the dis-ease and disharmony, whether that be physical, mental or spiritual. Supporting and empowering others to bring balance and harmony into their lives by learning to heal themselves and develop their spirituality brings Karolyn great joy and fulfilment.

Connect With Karolyn:

Website: www.krmtherapies.co.uk

Facebook: www.facebook.com/krmtherapies.co.uk.

'That Damned Curse is my Superpower'

By Fiona Dalziel

'I think we all have empathy. We may not have enough courage to display it.' ~ Maya Angelou

When I plucked up the courage to tell a 'friend' that I was seeing a counsellor for my mental health I am sure she thought I was making it up.

'You don't look like someone that needs therapy,' was her retort.

What does that even mean?

I don't even think she realised how that made me feel – I didn't tell anyone else for a very long time!

18 Months Earlier

After leaving my career in the corporate world due to a work-related breakdown, I will admit that I was naïve. I really did think that everything would be OK and that all the anxieties and stresses that I had been experiencing would just disappear, when in fact, they got worse.

Not immediately – there was the 'honeymoon period' when I was so euphoric at not having to go back to work. I was loving life – having dinner on the table for Mark, spending time with Natalie, our daughter, who was biding time before going off to university in the summer, driving about in my wee red Renault Clio (it was a bit of a novelty as getting rid of my Mercedes was part of the giving up work deal I had made with Mark), visiting friends, meeting up for lunch, and working for Oxfam tying up parcels to send to Indonesia after the tsunami. (I was a great Girl Guide and a packer's knot was my speciality. You see, I had tied a bedding roll or two in my life to date!)

The summer brought Natalie's 18th birthday and a whole host of parties and fun! Life was good, and I was getting better and better at putting on a great show. Don't get me wrong, while I had some fun times, there were some really dark times too.

I did some 'real work' doing a bit of restructuring and a little bit of recruitment. I even worked for a charity as a development officer. Life was feeling good. Despite some pretty ugly bouts of anxiety that I was in denial about at the time, I seemed to be coping.

The reality was quite a different story, and I didn't recognise that at the time. Looking back is a different picture entirely.

Mark and I argued a lot, I argued with Natalie a lot, and I began to think that life would be much easier if I wasn't around, which absolutely was not true.

My husband and my daughter were almost at a loss with what to do next – I was hysterical with tears and anxiety one moment and the next the world was great and I was absolutely fine. They didn't know when it was OK to leave me and when I needed to be watched.

Rock bottom wasn't far away though. I had almost reached my destination and it wasn't pretty.

I was so anxious that I used to drive myself to absolute insanity over the simplest things. If Mark wasn't home within 5-10 minutes of his normal time, I dreamt that he had died in a car crash or that he was lying in a ditch somewhere. Natalie, as a first year student at university, was stalked by me nearly every minute of the day, desperate to know she was safe, my heart racing and the redial button on my phone red hot from constantly calling until I got an answer.

Anxiety over what people thought of me and what I was doing, wearing, saying, was out of control.

I couldn't see how this was making life hell for myself and my family – not just watching me self-destruct but also not being able to relax at all when they were out of the house.

It all came to a head one Sunday in April. Mark and I had just returned from a few days holiday to Oban. Everything was relatively calm – no serious anxiety attacks. I had enjoyed some calm time and I was feeling much more like myself than I had in ages.

That morning, I woke up in a complete tizzy and it wasn't long before there was a full scale riot in the house. (Looking back, the trigger would have been there, however, I can't put my finger on what it was, no matter how hard I try. It is a moment in my life that I have tried to blank out so it isn't completely clear in my mind.)

I am not going to go into details here, maybe that is for another chapter in a book someday. For now, it is too painful and upsetting for all of us to go through again; we all remember it clearly as a reminder that it must never happen again. My amazing husband and daughter are my saviours and I love them dearly for being able to forgive me for what I put them through that day; they forgive me because they love me just as much in return.

Destination Rock Bottom

I needed help, not just another band aid, and I needed to admit that I wasn't OK.

This is the hardest thing I have ever had to do – I was broken, and I had absolutely nothing left after years of pretending.

Going into the doctor's surgery the next day, I was terrified – terrified that they were going to put me into a psychiatric hospital, terrified of being judged, terrified of being classed as weak and, most of all, terrified of admitting that I couldn't go on the way I was.

I was given an urgent appointment to see a psychologist on the Community Mental Health team the next afternoon. I was a nervous wreck – I didn't want to go; in fact, I had convinced myself I wasn't going.

I went. I went because, if there was one thing I knew at this stage, it was that I needed to go.

Bizarrely, one of the reasons I didn't want to go was because a friend was the practice manager in the health centre I was to visit. I entered the surgery like Inspector Clouseau just in case I needed to duck and dive. It was a ridiculous carry on, and I didn't even see her. I had managed to get away with it. All this going on in my life and yet still I was worried about what someone would think.

Jim the psychologist, who I eventually felt comfortable calling my counsellor, was so calming – whatever I was expecting, it wasn't this. Funnily, I still remember him wearing a brown round neck jumper, beige cords and desert boots – I have no idea why this is the detail I remember from that day!

I have absolutely no recollection of what we spoke about. I can only tell you two things about that meeting on top of what Jim was wearing – I felt listened to and I left with a workbook.

The workbook was my first step into CBT (Cognitive Behavioural Therapy) which was to last for 10 weeks. I worked through it on my own and with Jim to explore my feelings and reactions.

Now, I am not a counsellor or psychologist so please go easy on me if my facts are not 100 percent correct.

CBT helped me realise how my thoughts and beliefs made me feel and behave. It helped me to not listen to my inner self-talk, almost to talk back to it and tell it that it couldn't make me listen.

I really looked at how my anxiety was triggered and how it made me feel and the outcome of those feelings for me.

For example (and this was one of the lightbulb moments for me), worrying about Mark not being home or Natalie not answering her phone was not changing the outcome, and instead it triggered extreme anxiety which massively affected my behaviour.

Realising that worrying was the trigger for that particular situation and deciding not to worry or listen to my inner voice broke the chain reaction which would normally end in self-destructive behaviour.

I still use that framework today – it is part of my life.

This therapy, along with the professional help I received over the 10 weeks, had a profound impact on me. I put everything I had into it, supported by Mark and Natalie, and I repaid myself in dividends. It didn't completely heal me. It did, however, give me a foundation to rebuild myself on and a framework to do so.

After a three-month break, I returned for a further six weeks. This was really tough. There were many difficult conversations as we discovered where and when in my life this all began.

The Ugly Truth

I have always been a sensitive soul; I cry for many reasons and none.

In primary school, I cried for what was classed by my teachers as 'no reason'. I became known as 'Bubbly' and was bullied by three younger boys that lived round the corner from our house, although I was a bit of a laughing-stock in my own class too.

I used to dread school discos because I would get myself all worked up that no one was going to ask me to 'smoochy' dance with them – always to *Sailing* by Rod Stewart or *Sandy* by John Travolta from *Greece*. It was 1978 and they were the tunes of the moment. The tears would start as I stood at the edge of the dancefloor – more the fear of what others thought of me than not being 'picked' by one of the popular boys who were coming nowhere near me as I was 'Bubbly'. On one memorable occasion, I was so worked up that I picked a hole in the bottom of my polystyrene cup and ended up with cheap flat cola all over my new white trousers. Of course, everyone laughed and that led to more tears.

Moving to secondary school didn't make room for improvement with my sensitive feelings.

The first couple of years brought some moments of sheer hell as I struggled to control my emotions. My nickname had moved on from 'Bubbly' to 'Water Works' as, every time I found myself in a situation which required emotion, I cried, sometimes even when humour was called for.

It wasn't all bad news. There were some great fun times and one of those was a trip to Switzerland with the school where I found myself some new friends from the year below who accepted me for who I was; my confidence started to grow.

I developed a persona, a bolder, more confident act. I met a boy and, before long, he turned into a serious boyfriend; we were known around school as an item. This gave me even more confidence as I was Jimmy's girlfriend and not just 'Water Works'.

Don't get me wrong – there were still tears and emotion, I had just got better at hiding them.

And this is where it really started to go wrong. Sadly, it took me almost 30 years to discover this.

As I moved from school to further education, I became an Oscar-winning performer at playing a confident young woman. I played it so well, it felt like real life.

I worked in bars and clubs and was successful, vibrant and fun. This attracted lots of attention and looked from the outside like I was living the high life! Below the surface, I was still an emotional soul.

This confidence found me successfully working in the corporate world, a real go-getter moving and shaking in circles that would never have crossed my mind when I was younger; it did not portray my natural make-up of who I really was. And this was my downfall.

All these years of hiding 'the real me' in a box from the big wide world had come to a head.

The only person that got through this shell I had created was Mark, my husband. Not at first. In the early days of our relationship, I was courageous and volatile rolled into one, and yet he stayed despite the challenges. He loved me – and still loves me, unconditionally. I knew through these years of uncertainty in myself who I was and what I was doing. I threw everything at him, blamed him, scared him, and yet he held me tight and told me everything would be OK. He still does this when I get overwhelmed with emotion. He knew the real me even back then when I was living a lie to everyone else.

Learning to Understand My Tears

I cry if there is a christening in the church even if I don't know anyone involved. I cry if someone tells me about a member of their family being unwell, or if their gran's cat has passed away. For goodness' sake, I cry when I am recounting a story – happy or sad – or when my Guides make their Promise!

For a long time, I never understood this, and I was embarrassed about it.

Growing up as sensitive and empathetic I was made to feel oversensitive, too emotional. I was labelled as a cry baby and a wimp.

What was a real gift – my sensitive nature – was stifled to fit in with what was expected.

After my counselling with Jim was over, I spent a great deal of time looking from the outside in and making decisions built on how I felt. I spent time considering what I wanted for the rest of my life, together with my husband and our daughter.

One thing was certain – it could not go on the way it had for the past 20 years or more. I had to give up work completely and work solely on me.

I mentioned that I am a Girl Guide!

2010 brought the Girl Guiding Centenary celebrations and this incredible milestone was pivotal in my recovery. I became fully involved in preparations for many events in our local area and worked closely with my great friends Carol and Maureen. Spending time doing things I loved with people I really cared about and who understood my sensitive nature was an absolute joy and gave me space to think about what I wanted to do with my life – providing lots of opportunities for involuntary crying, might I add!

All my career I had worked against people rather than to help them – it was the nature of the beast. This no longer served me, and I felt proud of myself for realising this.

I started to study aromatherapy, something I had dabbled with in the past. I went to evening classes at my old high school – the one where all the trouble began – and, in a twist of fate, I ended up working in the office there for a short two-week stint. I stayed for four-and-a-half years! What can I say? I loved it! It was the best job I had ever had up until then, and the lowest paid job I had ever had too.

Big Changes Ahead

One evening in January 2016, Mark and I were sitting with a bottle of wine, chatting about what we really wanted from our life. We had a beautiful house, lovely holidays, we were so proud of our grown-up daughter – we really wanted for nothing. I made a comment that I would like to live on an island, one that was slightly smaller than mainland Britain. We laughed and gave it no more thought.

A month later, one Friday night, we were doing the same thing and Mark quipped, 'You know you said you would quite like to live on an island? Well, how about Orkney?' My first reaction was to say, 'Don't be ridiculous!' And then, as we talked it through, the thought became more attractive. (The company Mark worked for were bidding to build the island a new hospital and he had been asked if he would consider moving there for the duration of the project.)

We moved to Orkney in the week before Christmas 2016. The moment I set foot on that island I knew it would only bring good things for us.

Being part of an island community is a real privilege and the lovely people of Orkney welcomed us with open arms. Before long, I felt a real sense of belonging, a true feeling of home.

It was there that I first felt that the sensitivity that I had carried around like a damned curse most of my life was, in fact, my superpower. Now that I knew how to use it for the benefit of myself and others it would no longer be my nemesis.

I met a young woman called Kirsten. She was my podiatrist and we hit it off right away. She is a fellow empath – we walk the same road. We talked a lot about the holistic training I had done and what I was thinking of doing next, and she encouraged me. In fact, she even offered me a space to practice in her new place – the Hygge Clinic. You should visit if you are ever in Orkney!

Fiona Dalziel Holistic Therapy was born on that remote and beautiful island – a place in my heart forever. It was where I finally realised what my divine purpose is – to help other people heal and feel good about themselves.

My superpower makes me a far more intuitive healer. My depth of understanding of my clients' needs and my ability to read and feel their emotion has given me a whole new lease of life and allowed me to step into this passion and share it with the world.

I still cry for all reasons and none – I make no apologies, it's who I am, and I love that about me!

About the Author

Fiona Dalziel is an intuitive therapist, self-confessed empath and sensitive soul. These qualities are her trademark – her superpower! Embracing these sensitivities fuelled her passion to work with women to help them heal holistically – mind, body and soul – through her therapies. Fiona loves skin and believes that everyone has the right to natural beauty. Through her expert advice and natural skincare products, she helps women fall in love with their skin again.

From her therapy room in Alloa in Central Scotland, Fiona offers a range of indulgent and healing therapies, mindfulness coaching and guided meditation. Fiona is also the founder of Facepack, a successful Spa Facial at Home Subscription.

Connect With Fiona:

Website: www.fionadalziel.com
Facebook: www.facebook.com/fionadalzielholistictherapy
Instagram: www.instagram.com/thefacepackqueen

The Best is Yet to Come

By Mhairi Coleman

'If it is to be, it is up to me.' ~ William Johnsen

The morning of 26th May 2009 is etched in my mind forever.

I was home alone and getting ready for work. As I dried my hair, the radio playing in the background, thoughts raced through my mind. Another day of teaching. My gut churned at the prospect of the whispers and underhandedness of unsupportive peers which lay ahead.

There was a missed call on my mobile. It was my parents' number. *A call at this time?* Something was amiss. I returned the call. My brother answered. *Why was he answering so early in the morning?* 'We have lost Dad,' he said. 'What do mean we have lost Dad? Where is he?' I asked.

My heart immediately broke, a crushing pain in my chest like no other I'd ever experienced. I can still feel it to this day when I take myself back to that moment. I now know what a broken heart feels like.

I honestly didn't think I'd feel that way. I'd spent a lot of time avoiding my father as I didn't find it easy to talk to him; we didn't spend a lot of time together as he worked hard so I spent a lot of time with Mum. I respected, loved and feared Dad all at once, only wanting to make him proud and gain his approval. I never felt worthy and put that down to my insecurities of not being as smart or hard working as my older sister. None of which was true of course, as we are all individuals – I have always done 'me' and not tried to be anyone else – but I still had that comparison gremlin inside.

Rewind to the autumn of 1995. I decided I wanted to improve my prospects, join the Royal Navy and become more independent – staying in my hometown was not going to fulfil my desire to travel or escape the small town mentality, or make my own way in life. My father had been a police constable and I thought he'd be pleased that I was looking at a stable career. I had to break the news of my plans to my parents but only once I knew I'd passed an entry exam and medical – there was no point rocking the boat unless I was successful.

The time came one evening at the dinner table. 'I've got something to tell you,' I said. Tell being the word, not ask. I could see the worse-case scenarios going through Dad's head. Telling him that I wanted to join the Royal Navy might as well have been as bad. The news went down like a lead balloon! I explained my logic of bed, board and education all in one. I was 21 – I'd made my decision. So, in March the following year, I joined HMS Raleigh for basic training and successfully completed over 12 years' service (and also gained a diagnosis of dyslexia).

Our father's premature passing had been a huge shock to the whole family and our community. A fit and active man in his late 60s, he had a heart attack and was found on farmland (with the help of Moffat Mountain Rescue and Dumfries & Galloway Constabulary) on the morning of my brother's call. My immediate thoughts were that I needed to be with my mum and siblings. A call to my older sister sealed the agreement to travel 'home' together.

I contacted my husband who was at sea for the day to share my grief-stricken news. I informed work of my bereavement then travelled with my sister and her family to our family home, relieved that I did not have to go into work. My young nephew, who was wise beyond his years, reached out his hand to mine from his car seat and told me, 'It'll be okay, Auntie Mhairi.'

Beyond the Sea

The previous year, I had made the bold decision to apply for a career in further education – good salary and holidays, stability, another good pension and closer to home. By now, I was based in Scotland and had a home in Stirlingshire. What more could I want other than a family of my own?

Watching the 2008 Olympics with my husband while on a relaxing weekend away at Gleneagles, my mobile rang. It was a job offer for what seemed like a dream career following on from my military service. Quickly, I set about leaving my dental career in the Royal Navy, giving a month's notice as opposed to the standard twelve and forfeiting all resettlement training. As I already held appropriate and transferable qualifications, and with a new teaching qualification to come, that to me was worth the sacrifice.

I quickly adapted to civilian life once again, commuting early to miss traffic congestion, teaching evening classes, arriving home late and preparing lessons for the days and weeks ahead. This was no easy task as an adult who'd been diagnosed with dyslexia in my early 30s.

I felt unsupported in my new role. I had a lot to learn, a new environment to contend with, but felt I was doing well considering the lack of team support and apparent bitterness that I'd been given the post over a part-time colleague and friend. The PowerPoint lessons were not being shared with me, despite the curriculum being taught by senior, more experienced lecturers for many years before. So, I had to recreate them myself. I was chasing my tail, preparing a lesson to then teach it, then preparing another to teach, spending my weekends trying to get a step ahead! I turned Friday evenings into my weekend, going out for dinner with my husband, and spent Saturdays and Sundays planning lessons and preparing more PowerPoint presentations. I made sure I was at work early to secure the teaching aids required, only to find that they were not where they should be or that they were hidden (and yes, I did find hidden equipment). I think I went down a dress size with the stress, lack of support, and the cruel, petty and childlike behaviours.

The last weekend I saw my parents together was when they were returning from a longer cruise than experienced before. I knew they would be at my sister's house on Sunday so, instead of making Friday evening my weekend, I switched it to all day Sunday so that I could see them. I got to have my last and most comfortable conversation with Dad on his own while he watched the Grand Prix. He shared his holiday highlights and delight to be home once again. That decision to change days was pivotal – if I hadn't, I would have regretted putting work before family for the rest of my life.

After the painful loss of the man I respected and looked up to, I decided that I was not going to tolerate what I was suffering in my workplace. I did not want to be surrounded by bitter, jealous and negative energies while battling to be heard. No longer having the strength after the loss of Dad to fight, I resigned.

I took time out to find myself again, to spend time with our mum and re-evaluate what was important to me. I decided that it was time to try for my own family, look after my own health, and become the best version of me.

After a period of time, I applied for two NHS dental jobs and was successful in both applications – I took both roles to try to replace my lecturing salary! The first was working unsociable hours and the other was full-time, giving me an insight into areas of dentistry I wanted to get more involved in. I was particularly passionate about working alongside dental undergraduates and with 'Childsmile', a national programme to improve the oral health of children in Scotland.

Having gained qualifications in oral health and nutrition and health, I was able to transfer service to my local health board in Forth Valley, after successfully passing an interview for a term-time contract which gave me the school holidays to catch up with friends and family. It was the perfect contract if I was to continue to work, should I have a family. This made me happy until I fell into the trap of working six days a week, no longer seeing family on weekends and having to work Christmas and other public holidays. I did this for over five years. My health began to suffer, stress levels rose, I had unsuccessful attempts to carry a baby, and I dreaded the intense weekend shifts.

Forever Grateful

While enjoying an extended summer holiday, an ex-military colleague shared what she'd been doing after finishing her military career. She knew I was passionate about health and wellness from working together and also how unhappy I was with my current work pattern and my desire to become a mother. She presented an opportunity to be in control of my own destiny and help others at the same time. I knew I had nothing to lose and everything to gain. I started my business – Mhairi Coleman Your Wellness in Mind – in 2015 under the umbrella of a successful international company. I believed that, if I could recommend the health and wellness products I'd fallen in love with to my family and friends, I'd satisfy my desire to help myself and others while replacing my weekend income.

Soon, I achieved what I set out to do. I escaped the torture of my weekend contract – the weight on my shoulders was immediately lifted. I was starting to get the flexibility I craved and I was feeling better – I didn't look back! Focusing on my mindset and the positive influence of my new business partners, I continued to develop myself personally and professionally. No longer was my focus on my dental career but instead on my passion to help others look and feel better, in the same way that I had helped myself. Not long after, my dream came true. Aged 41, I conceived our daughter. I had a very healthy 'geriatric' pregnancy and birthed the most precious and perfect gift which I'm eternally grateful for.

I took a year of maternity leave followed by a career break. I fully embraced motherhood, relished the time with our daughter and was one hundred percent there for her in her early years as I always hoped I would be. Being there for all of her 'firsts' and sharing her with family and friends has been an absolute joy. I enjoyed the groups, friendships made and networking with others but felt sad knowing what Dad was missing. I know he would be proud, happy and would have loved her as much as we all do. As an older mum, I feel strong and secure in my abilities with all the life experiences and challenges I have had which has helped me to push on through and grow.

During this time, knowing I'm an older mum, I knew that I didn't want to work forever and miss our daughter growing up to find that I'd missed her milestones or any precious time together. Reading Dad's diaries, I remembered the long hours he worked between his police service and farming. He did it for his family but didn't get to enjoy the rewards of his labour in later life. If I can take anything from losing him, it is to keep as healthy as possible. I don't want to work until I'm in my 60s in a traditional job and then potentially die. Life is for living and having fun and that's what my business gives me – health, fun, hope and optimism for a better work-life balance.

2020 was the year that a global pandemic rocked our world. I have never been more grateful for the pandemic-proof business I have grown and was able to continue to support the immune health of myself and others and their income when their traditional businesses were mothballed.

Returning to the NHS during the pandemic was an experience like no other. I joined a Covid-19 testing team – all of us stepping into the unknown – but the most wonderful team who gave their all and more. The pain, sadness and pressure on all areas of care will never leave me but the joy of new friendships and a camaraderie of a different kind from the military made the experience positively memorable.

In business I started to take on challenges to further develop myself and help my business grow. I joined and became a member of an amazing group for women in business on Facebook who I've built great friendships with, and have gone on to meet these friends and fellow business owners in person. I also met Katherine Massey, the host of this amazing book collaboration, online while learning more about Instagram and LinkedIn, soon joining her online Road Trip to Visibility and becoming confident to go live on social media. I became a member of her VQ Academy and I am continually inspired and encouraged to grow.

My goal since starting my new life has been to help and inspire others to look after their health and grow personally and professionally. I have my clients' health and happiness in the forefront of my mind and aim to supply the highest quality wellness products to health seeking individuals, helping them to look and feel better when they think there is no other way. I mentor conscious and committed individuals from all walks of life to grow their own business, enabling them to become happy and fulfilled on their own terms. I support these journeys with vigour and integrity.

My focus has never waned. My nephew was correct – everything *is* okay and continues to be so. And I know the very best is yet to come!

'Take care of your body. It's the only place you have to live.'
~ Jim Rohn

About the Author

Mhairi Coleman is a health and wellness mentor, and believer in nature for helping others to look and feel better. A quietly confident, busy mum of one, Mhairi lives with intention and is passionate about helping others to become happy and fulfilled on their own terms. With a military background and over 25 years in dentistry, Mhairi has followed her true passion of health and nutrition and has her clients' overall wellness at the centre of what she does.

Genuine, caring and approachable, nothing gives Mhairi more pleasure than helping others to achieve success on a personal or professional level. Providing a personal and tailored service, Mhairi builds loyalty, respect and trust.

Connect with Mhairi:

Facebook: www.facebook.com/mfcyourwellnessinmind
Instagram: www.instagram.com/mfcflp
LinkedIn: www.linkedin.com/in/mhairi-coleman
Linktree: www.linktr.ee/mhairicoleman

From Setback to Comeback QUEEN

By Josephine Sandra Kalagira

God has already arranged a comeback for every setback, a vindication for every wrong and a new beginning for every disappointment.

I vividly remember the morning.

I woke up to get my son ready for school. Almost instantly, as I tried to remove my duvet so I could roll out of bed, I noticed that something wasn't right; I couldn't do it. I wondered what was going on. I couldn't feel the right side of my body and my left side felt so weak. I tried to roll out of bed but I was in so much pain, more than I could bear. Even though I was already in pain due to an ongoing health condition, this was different. The more I forced my body to move, the more pain sensations, pins and needles and uncontrollable shaking I felt. My body felt like a heavy load. In that moment, there was nothing I could physically do to help my son get ready for school. The taxi that was waiting to take him drove away because he had not got out on time, and I had no choice but to call the school to let them know that my son would not be in today. Realising how much I was letting him down broke my heart.

In this chapter, I'm going to explain and address functional neurological disorder (FND) and symptoms of complex regional pain syndrome (CRPS) – my health condition – because I believe you can join me in helping to spread awareness. FND is a problem with the functioning of the nervous system and how the brain and the body send or receive signals. Neurological symptoms range from paralysis, weakness, fits, seizures, fatigue, sensory issues, gait issues, and so much more. Functional systems are the second most common reason for a neurology consultation after that of a headache. It is not widely known but neurological disorders, such as functional movement disorders or functional seizures, account for six percent of referrals. That's more than Parkinson's disease at five percent or multiple sclerosis (MS) at four percent. Due to the misconception about FND I feel called to raise awareness and support those affected, including the professionals helping to treat not only those who battle with FND but their friends, family, co-workers and communities, and educate about how disabling FND can be, wreaking havoc and financial chaos on families.

FND can happen to anyone at any time of their lives. Due to the complexity of the condition, you may feel drained and frustrated when figuring out the root cause. I have found that we underestimate anything that happens to us, but you should not. For me, all of the health complications started after a collision with a fully loaded cage in my local supermarket, long before I was diagnosed with FND.

A Vicious Cycle of Pain and Medication

After the impact with the cage, I instantly felt pain in my right leg, foot and ankle, which had twisted inwards as I was wearing high-heeled shoes. I wobbled but fortunately didn't fall on the floor. I felt dizzy and confused, embarrassed even. The staff member who hit me said sorry; I believe he realised that he was at fault. My son, aged five at the time, was with me when I got injured. I tried to pretend that I wasn't hurt. My son in his little voice said, 'I'm so sorry Mum, I did not save you.' Bless him. From this point, what I call the devil started creeping up on me. I tried to be strong and pretend that everything was fine but the more I tried to walk around (as I wanted to continue shopping), the more difficult it became. The pain was getting sharper and unbearable. I leaped to the door where the staff member whose cage had hit me had entered. When he saw me, he hid under a table. I went to the customer service desk to ask for someone in charge. I was told that, as they were busy serving other customers, I needed to stand at the side and wait for the manager to be called.

To my surprise, the person who was called was the person who had hit me. He was the manager of the store. He opened another till and began serving other customers in the queue. I went closer and said to him that I wanted to have a word. Even though my son was playing around and I was standing right beside the till, the manager pretended not to see me. Despite my efforts to talk to him, he ignored me. This is when I demanded to know how to make a complaint about the incident. The manager immediately responded with a dismissive, 'On your way out there are leaflets.' I pointed out that he was directing me to a stack of catalogues – nothing to do with complaint forms to report an injury. He never responded. I stormed out of the store, grabbing a couple of catalogues in anger. I recall being in so much pain and being treated with no duty of care. I dropped some of my shopping; my son helped to pick it up for me.

When I sat in the car, I looked through the catalogues and found a customer service number that I rang to report what had happened. They were concerned and apologised, informing me that they were going to investigate. My complaint was verified after a couple of months. The store's member of staff had injured me hence they were liable. However, this did not resolve my increasing health issues. Yes, I managed to get home that day, although I stalled the car several times, but, despite taking pain killers, the agony never settled. My foot was increasingly swelling, throbbing and tingling. I called the out-of-hours doctor to explain the symptoms I was experiencing and was advised to go to A&E immediately. By this point, I did not dare to drive so asked someone to take me to the hospital.

Throughout the journey to hospital and up until when I was seen by the doctor, I felt like I was in another world, experiencing what felt like labour contractions. I was examined visually but no X-rays were done. According to the specialist on duty, it was a soft tissue injury and the pain and swelling would reduce in 72 hours. I was advised to take pain killers every four hours, rest and sleep with my foot raised. And that was it. Due to the level of pain, I did not feel satisfied that no X-rays were done. However, I did not want to appear to be doubting the specialist. At home, despite taking regular pain killers and doing everything that was recommended, I did not sleep well. I was so restless. I could not weight-bear either. I wanted to go back to the hospital but decided to wait until 72 hours had passed. When my symptoms did not show any signs of improvement I revisited the hospital. Again, I was not X-rayed but was given crutches and told to contact my doctor for further treatment.

This is when my depressive journey began. Despite going to the doctor's surgery repeatedly for more medication and sick notes, visiting time was limited; I barely had time to express myself the way I really wanted to. I was in so much physical and emotional pain that I spent most of the time in tears and unable to articulate what I wanted to say. This encouraged the professionals to prescribe more medication. The medication alone came with lots of side effects like sleepless nights, lack of concentration and weight gain, but the pain only eased with heavy doses so I had little choice but to take them. At this point, I could neither stand unaided nor drive. As a single parent, I really hoped that things would get better soon so I decided to use taxis to take my son to school as it was quite a distance. The cost was high. For a taxi to collect me from home and take me to my son's school plus waiting time charges was a minimum of £25 per day.

While coming to terms with my declining health, I got a call from work asking me to go and see an occupational therapist to identify how they could help me to get back to work. Every time I spoke with my manager I kept promising that everything was going to be okay; deep down I knew I was over-stretching myself. I was working full-time, nearly an hour away from home, so getting to work was a challenge now that I couldn't drive and the train station was quite a distance, on top of what I was already paying for my son's school pick-up and drop-off. Eventually, even though this was my dream job and I was planning to move closer to the office, I was told that my job was no more. My absence had caused such a detrimental impact on the team.

When my job ended, I started to feel the dent financially, having used all of my personal savings and my son's. I turned to benefits. By now, my mobility was getting worse; pain was moving up my leg, a leg that no longer felt like my own and which felt heavy to carry. I struggled to move from one room in my house to another. I was prone to falling and having panic attacks. My confidence was knocked, I had low self-esteem, and could hardly remember my self-worth. My son witnessed everything I was going through, helping me to do some house chores, witnessing my attacks and falls, and helping me into the bathroom. I felt so guilty that the situation I was going through not only impacted me but also my son, depriving him of being a proper child. He lost friends as I couldn't physically take him to see them; he fell behind in class because I could not emotionally support him with his homework which impacted his well-being even though he put on a brave face. My son hated going to school because he thought that, if he did, he would come home to find me dead because of the episodes he had witnessed.

With everything I was going through, I didn't see myself getting better. We hardly had food to eat, and at one time we did not even have gas and electricity. What was heart-breaking was that, at my lowest, I asked to borrow some money for gas and electricity from someone who I thought would help me. It was only twenty pounds and I promised to pay her back. She said no. I burst into tears, screamed out loud and thought to myself that I would be better off dead. I told her I would not make it to the following day and threw the phone at the wall. That's when I developed the idea to take my own life. (I tried to a few times, but thankfully failed.) Strangely, the person that I trusted who refused to lend me the money called me from an anonymous number the following day. I picked up. After saying hello, the caller responded, 'So, you are still alive then?' I thanked her and said, 'Yes, I am.' She kept quiet and hung up. This demonstrated how people can treat others in need; I learned a lot from this.

I was forcing myself to feel better but really I felt terrible. I struggled daily with the simplest of activities like cooking, being a good mum, cleaning, and taking myself to the bathroom. I put off seeking help, worried about what everyone would say and think of me, but the more I did this, the more my son and I were affected.

One day, things got out of hand. I had sworn not to become wheelchair bound but on 16th December 2019, I slipped and fell heavily. I was using crutches at the time and, as I tried to stop myself from landing on the floor, I twisted my right hand, hit the wall and lost balance. I landed on the tiled concrete, my head hitting a metallic rail. I was on the floor for over two hours waiting for the ambulance to come while the whole neighbourhood stood around, making sure I was okay. Honestly, I have never been so embarrassed in my life! I was taken to hospital who determined that, due to my ongoing chronic pain and FND, there was nothing they could do beyond the medication I was on.

It was a morning in March 2020, at the beginning of lockdown, that I woke up, unable to get out of bed. After calling the school to tell them what was going on and that my son wouldn't be going in, they informed his family practitioner who came to ensure that we were both okay. The family practitioner advised me to call my doctor to get monitored and review my medication.

Well, upon calling the doctor she concluded on the call that I had lost the plot. She said, 'To be quite honest Josephine, you are not coping, your depression is getting worse, and that's it. I'm hanging up to call emergency social care services to come and get your son to take him where he will be very well looked after because clearly you are not coping.' I was in tears. Before saying another word, the doctor had hung up on me. Fortunately, I was already in contact with social services. I contacted them about what had happened and they waited to be contacted by the doctor, advising her that they were aware of my situation and were supporting me. This went in my favour. I also wrote to the surgery to explain what had happened and how it had impacted me. In the end, I was given an apology for how the doctor had conducted the call.

The BPS Framework Model

Here's the thing, nothing will ever prepare you for any challenge in your life, whether a physical or emotional one. Whatever you are experiencing, struggling with, and battling through is what I call a setback but not the end of life. It could be that you are trying to have the fruit of the womb. Perhaps you have had an accident that you thought you would heal from but are still impacted by. Maybe you are looking for justice in your life or you wish people would treat you better. Perhaps you want to be the best mum but feel you are failing. Maybe you have lost friends, have no job, or feel like you are being judged, unheard and unsupported. Perhaps you are constantly in pain or feeling hopeless with so much confusion about your purpose in life.

It is very easy to say that 'life is not fair' and yes, life isn't fair. But I've learnt – life is what you make it.

I wanted to make a positive change despite my health challenges so that I could take ownership of my life and become the best mum for my son. I knew it was not going to be easy but was determined to find the strength to make things happen. I did not want to live this way for the rest of my life. I kept thinking, *if I am going to die, at least let me die trying.*

My general health was a product of several aspects of my life overlapping and interplaying with one another. After an insightful self-discovery and personal development journey, I was able to create the enlightened BPS (Biopsychosocial) Framework Model which focussed on enabling me to start identifying the various factors that contributed to my challenges, struggles, pain, disability, and frustrations. This transformed my life. Even now, I use the framework to get back on track and stay focussed without feeling overwhelmed. In fact, that was one of the inspirations to write my first book, *The Revolutionary Breakthrough: How To Turn Your Setback into a Purposeful Comeback* as well as contributing to another collaboration, *Love Thy Body Volume One,* both within one year. The feedback I received gave me the confidence, strength, resilience, and motivation to step into my PASSION, PURPOSE and POWER. I have been able to help others on a similar journey, those who have said YES to investing in themselves to transform their lives through mentoring, coaching, or being supported by me. When I share my pearls of wisdom using this model to everyone who have put their trust in me, they say, 'Josephine, where have you been all my life?'!

My advice to you right now, as the 'Setback to Comeback Queen', is to never give up. Ever. Never take 'no' for an answer if you know what's right for you. Don't go with the flock to make others happy when you are not. Always reach out and seek help that is tailored to you. Understand that you are the author of your story or experience. Know your value and understand your worth; what you are going through or have been through cannot define the person you are if you do not allow it. Even though you have been let down or not believed in, there will always be a safe space for you to feel heard, accepted and supported – never think you are alone. Fight for what's yours to make positive changes in your life.

I was able to achieve all of the above and more. My son is now so much happier and stronger than ever, and we both have the strongest bond with zero regrets and no self-blaming – we are no longer living in silence or fear, and he is so proud of my achievements.

If I can come back from a setback, so can you.

About the Author

Josephine Sandra Kalagira, aka the 'Setback to Comeback Queen', is a mother, author, speaker, and empowerment mentor. She believes that we can overcome adversity when we can identify and accept that there is no reason bigger than ourselves to compel us never to give up on following our dreams.

Josephine believes by accepting and embracing who we really are and what we have been through that will allow us to become empowered and learn to take ownership of our lives. As a result of her lived experience, Josephine felt called to share her story, lessons, advice and tips to support others living with physical or emotional adversities, helping them turn their setbacks into their comeback!

Connect with Josephine:

Website: www.josephinesandracoaching.co.uk
Facebook:
www.facebook.com/groups/thriveandshinethroughyoursetbacks
Email: Josephinekalagira@gmail.com

My Greatest Superpower

By Dee O'Connor

'The intuitive mind is a sacred gift and the rational mind is a faithful servant. We have created a society that honours the servant and has forgotten the gift.' ~ Albert Einstein

Your greatest superpower, if you haven't learnt to tap into it yet, is your intuition. You can fine tune it to be the greatest conductor of your life; everyone has the ability to access it when they learn how. It is our natural way of being to follow our inner guidance and intuition, but too often we unknowingly allow our minds to be hijacked by the self-limiting beliefs from our subconscious mind. Intuition is our true innate power that many recognise as that inner knowing or gut instinct.

Fear can be the biggest killer of dreams, leaving many of us unable to reach our true potential. We allow fear to be the pilot of our central navigation systems – our subconscious mind is responsible for 80-90 percent of decisions that we make – leaving us surviving instead of thriving. But I'm here to tell you it doesn't always have to be that way. Living a life fearfully can have a detrimental effect on your health and wellbeing, impacting your nervous system and causing chronic stress, depression and disease (dis-ease in the body). But you CAN take back control of your life. You CAN get back in the driving seat and navigate your life. You can re-write the script by uncovering these ingrained beliefs.

These limiting beliefs can come from experiences in our life. They can be cultural, religious, genetic or even collective beliefs taken on from others. We form many of our beliefs in our early years which are perceived through the mind of our child self and they often still play out in adulthood.

'Yesterday I was clever, so I wanted to change the world. Today I am wise, so I am changing myself.' ~ Rumi

Did you know that life reflects back at you the beliefs that you carry? What self-imposed limitations has your inner critic placed upon itself? Where have you given your power away? Our brain is like a supercomputer and we can upgrade our beliefs whenever we want. Our beliefs become our reality and our experiences shape who we are. If you keep repeating cycles of limiting beliefs you will create that reality for yourself, as you will keep attracting situations that mirror that belief until it is healed.

Beliefs held in our sub-conscious are transformed and changed to empowering and positive beliefs whilst in a theta brainwave when you are in a deep relaxed state. These beliefs can be so deeply ingrained within us that they remain invisible until we bring them into our conscious awareness to heal. Beliefs like 'I'm not good enough', 'I'm stupid' or, 'I'm a failure' will leave you feeling worthless, leading to self-doubt, low self-esteem and lack of self-confidence. Is your inner voice kind and compassionate or is it harsh and critical? Would you talk to someone you love like that? Your subconscious mind is always trying to keep you safe and protect you but it can dominate your life based on your belief systems. It's important to know how the mind works, create new neural pathways and release any thought forms that have negatively charged emotions. Your mind can be your best friend or your worst enemy.

Fear of Being Seen

'Of all the liars in the world, sometimes the worst are our own fears.' ~ Rudyard Kipling

I have taken multiple courses over several years and learnt many skills and tools along the way, working at a high level and helping others where I could ... but never putting myself out there publicly. After having a big panic attack while writing this chapter realising that I would soon be *Seen*, it occurred to me that I had intended to step out many times in the past with all my gifts and talents – but I kept finding reasons to stay within my comfort zone. My subconscious mind had done an amazing job of convincing me that I had another skill to learn or something to perfect. I had gone from course to course learning valuable skills and tools but something always stopped me from moving forward and being visible with my business. I had not recognised the good old belief that was holding me prisoner – 'I am not enough'. My subconscious mind had worked tirelessly convincing me that I wasn't ready – fear and doubt are the biggest killer of dreams. The reality was that I was very capable! I was subconsciously staying in my comfort zone and protecting myself from all the emotions that would arise if I stepped out. There was something unresolved that needed healing and my mind was saying, *oh no you don't, it's not safe.*

As quick as this fear tried to take control, I realised this could be the last page of an old story that I could tear up and re-write the ending. I had the power and the tools to change these feelings and emotions. I remembered the reason why I had wanted to be a part of this book and I had not hesitated when I knew it was to support mental health. This wasn't about me! It was about others. Hadn't I always wanted to help others? That was enough for me to take back control. I had my WHY.

I silenced that monkey mind – we can create all sorts of stories and illusions to protect ourselves when we are in fear. I connected into this fear and found myself asking, *where is it coming from? What am I getting out of it? When did it even start? Why was it creating so much fear to be seen?*

My intuition was back in the driving seat. I could have allowed that fear to control me but I had the power to change it and take back control. I had shifted my mindset and stopped my subconscious mind from preventing me from moving forward.

'I learned that courage was not the absence of fear but the triumph over it.' ~ Nelson Mandela

I'm so very grateful that I have the tools to not only empower myself and my family but to also help others live their best lives. In order to truly help others as much as I had wanted, I needed to put my oxygen mask on first and heal fully to be of greater support to others – I had overcome this final hurdle. I had gone through a traumatic bullying experience some years ago, which had knocked my confidence and affected my health, and healed as far as I had allowed at that point. It's only in writing this chapter and truly feeling the fear of being seen come to the surface that I was truly able to heal. Experiences can have enormous impact on our wellbeing and our subconscious is always doing its best to protect us, whether it is right for us or not.

Some of us carry trauma right back to our birth; perhaps we had a traumatic delivery and we can carry this trauma through our lives. I was born with a cord wrapped round my neck which left me quite an anxious baby with lots of digestive issues, stomach complaints and colic. It was important for me to release that traumatic experience from my subconscious; otherwise, the world would always seem fearful and dangerous if fighting for breath was my first experience. (It has also been scientifically proven that trauma experienced by our ancestors is held in our DNA, with traumatic experiences being passed down through generations.)

My first memories of feeling anxious was when I started full-time education at the age of five. I managed as best as I could and did well with classwork but struggled with confidence. I had poor memory recall so I found exams and trying to retain so much information overwhelming. I was the sort of student that, if you handed me a project I would get an A*, but if you gave me a written exam – not so good! I was always worried about failing and I became sick with glandular fever right before my O Level exams. This pattern followed in later life when taking other exams. I would repeatedly become unwell with tonsilitis and other illnesses due to stress about not being good enough and the fear of not being able to remember everything.

Many children struggle at school as they have different ways of learning and they don't always fit into the box. This often leads to frustration, low self-esteem and anxiety. I've seen many children become depressed and have low self-worth from years of struggling at school. Imagine if the next generation were supported educationally in school with their emotional health and this subject was made a priority. Imagine if they were given the tools to empower themselves to promote balance and a positive mindset at a young age to reach their true potential. After all, happiness comes from within and happiness boosts performance!

Simple practices such as gratitude increase energy, reduce anxiety, improve sleep, focus attention, happiness and peace, and redirect your mind in a positive way. Meditation has enormous benefits such as improving focus, concentration and clarity, reducing stress levels and boosting the immune system. Meditation is like a massage for the brain. More people are open to meditation than ever before – artists realise how meditation can boost their creativity, while high performers and athletes visualise themselves achieving success over and over again until it becomes such a reality that it accelerates their performance. Visualisations in our mind are incredibly powerful – your mind doesn't know the difference between what is real and what is imaginary.

I danced a lot as a child and absolutely loved it! But I insisted I would never do competitions. That didn't last very long as I completely fell in love with Irish dancing and, within a year, I was doing really well in major dancing competitions. As I entered bigger competitions, anxiety reared its ugly head. The mornings would start with stomach pains and, by the time I was ready to walk on stage, my legs would either feel like jelly or turn to lead. I managed it mostly and always pushed through as I loved it so much, but when I went to the world championships I found the crowds incredibly overwhelming. I never performed as well as I could, no matter how hard I had worked beforehand. As a teenager, I went to college to do a private secretarial course. Having found exams stressful, I didn't want to pursue A Levels. So, this was the beginning of staying in my comfort zone.

I worked in the City for eighteen years for law firms doing legal secretarial work and I married at 27. After five years of infertility I was blessed with two beautiful boys. And they honestly are my greatest achievement in life. I had sought out a reflexologist for my fertility issues which was my first introduction to energy work and soon became fascinated with how it assisted relaxation and brought balance to the body. I had experienced many miscarriages in between both of my children plus several after my second son was born and, although I felt utterly blessed, my self-esteem and confidence had taken quite a knocking. I found myself wanting to explore more energy work and became fascinated with Reiki. And so the journey of self-development and training in Reiki and many healing modalities including life coaching, NLP (neuro linguistic programming) and CBT (cognitive behaviour therapy) began.

Something I definitely learned on my journey was that self-love is not selfish. I was definitely an over-giver and a people-pleaser, believing I had to always put myself last – I thought that was love. But I would leave myself depleted and exhausted. I have learnt along the way that the most important relationship you will ever have is the one you have with yourself. If you have the belief that love is sacrifice, you can leave yourself feeling neglected with no boundaries and little self-value. But the most important thing is that you can be kind – kind to yourself. You have to be able to set boundaries and have someone honour your feelings.

Reclaiming Your Power

'Don't let the noise of others' opinions drown out your inner voice.' ~ Steve Jobs

When someone tries to destroy your reputation because you stand up to their bullying and toxic behaviour towards you, it can cause deep emotional trauma and feelings of betrayal, hurt and pain. It is particularly traumatising when there is no remorse shown which is difficult to comprehend.

It is quite heart-breaking when you are targeted because others are full of anger and hatred. But as cruel as these experiences were for me, and as much as they were painful, I learnt to see the truth behind others' behaviour and see that people can project their own unhappiness onto others – it wasn't about me. And I had to stop defining myself by their behaviour and take my power back. Sometimes these wounds can run deep and these experiences caused my body to go into shock. My thyroid health declined and I piled on over three stone in weight, increasing my lack of self-confidence.

Looking back, the only advice I can give you is to not attach your self-worth to something outside of yourself, nor be defined by other people's behaviour. Don't give that power to others. We need to do the work to overcome certain things in our lives. I was a hostage to what other people thought of me. I allowed myself to be traumatised by ugly lies, malicious gossip and defamation of my character. I decided to look at all the beliefs that may have attracted those painful experiences into my life and heal those wounds.

As painful as situations are, we are always learning something. The people that the bullying removed from my life were replaced with the kindest, most loyal friends and the most amazing humans I could ever meet. I became stronger than ever and I learned how to stand up for myself which I had not been very good at before. I learnt that I had a choice to hold on to anger, bitterness and resentment, or I could heal and understand *why* people behave the way they behave, recognising that they are operating from their own wounded self.

There is true power by healing those traumas and letting go of any resentment. Pain, anger and toxic thoughts only leave you bitter. They only hurt YOU, weakening your immune system and ultimately leading to unhappiness, pain and illness. So, forgiveness is freedom for *you*. Forgiveness is NOT saying that someone's behaviour or what they did to you is OK; it is simply saying that you don't have to hold on to that emotion and give it power anymore. Love and happiness are your superpower and love is definitely more powerful than hate will ever be. But if someone is affecting your mental health and causing you pain, then you have a right to set boundaries on how you wish to be treated.

Once we truly understand what is going on for somebody and where they are operating from, we can see things through a different lens and give less power to their words or beliefs, realising that they are operating from their own unhappiness.

I didn't always listen to my intuition. There were valuable lessons, even if painful, teaching me to stay away from those that do not want the best for me. I learned that you can't *make* people like you, no matter how kind you are, and if something doesn't feel right, trust it. I learned to only focus energy on those that will love you unconditionally. I am grateful that these situations taught me to listen to that gut feeling and to not ignore my intuition.

All you can do is grow from your experiences; every one is teaching you something. Toxic emotions such as jealousy and greed are like a cancer, and I learnt you can't change others unless they are ready to change themselves (and they are not always willing). You can only change how you respond.

Surround yourself with those who genuinely care for you and allow you to speak your truth without ostracising you for having boundaries. It was never love if it was conditional on them controlling you. Love is unconditional. Not everyone will apologise and own their behaviour but forgive them anyway so that it doesn't hurt you. Always honour yourself and set healthy boundaries for how you wish to be treated. Live with integrity and stay true to yourself because love is also your superpower.

I am a very different person to when I started my journey. I see life through a different lens. Everything I have gone through I am grateful for the lessons. And anyone that hurt me, well, I thank them as they were my greatest teachers. I healed myself until I felt nothing but compassion and forgiveness. That doesn't mean that what they did to me was OK. It means I chose to let go of that pain, anger and hurt in my body, pain that would otherwise hurt *me.* Remember, unresolved emotions lead to dis-ease and imbalance if left unhealed.

So, if fear has been your friend, take your power back. Be authentic and don't change to fit in or please others. You are meant to be unique. You *are* magnificent.

About the Author

Dee O'Connor is an empowerment coach for kids, teens and adults. She is a master in Rahanni, Usui Reiki and is an Angelic Reiki teacher. She is also a meditation teacher certified in CBT, NLP, hypnotherapy, mindfulness and life coaching. Dee has trained in many healing modalities such as theta healing, EFT, emotional release, access bars, crystal healing and reflexology, and is a Young Living essential oils and Rain Seed Nutrition distributor.

Dee is a naturally gifted and talented energy healer and coach who is passionate about empowering those who have lost their confidence and self-esteem by helping them to overcome their limiting beliefs in order to step into their power and reach their true potential. Dee supports her clients to become happy, balanced, positive and confident individuals and to know that they are enough. She radiates a warmth that makes others feel supported, cared for and safe.

Connect With Dee:

Website: www.deemoconnor.com
Email: dee@deemoconnor.com

I Showed Up

By Susan Miller

'Dear Susan, my 7th granddaughter.
So according to fortune teller's predictions - she must be a gifted child. We will expect much good to come of your life.'
~ Love Grandma Stuart

I received an 'autograph book' for my 10th birthday so was eagerly getting family and friends to write something in it. Most of the comments were silly or benign – but one entry has stuck in my head for 40 years and I've found myself trying to live up to it ever since.

For more years than I can remember, my brain will periodically flick to words I can hear my grandma saying. You know when a line and melody from a song lyric suddenly pops into your head for no reason and it's so hard to get rid of it? An 'earworm' they call it. That's how I can describe it.

'I'm the 7th granddaughter … I'm gifted … Much good is expected…'

Strangely, it was only a few months ago when I was clearing out boxes in our garage that this very autograph book just appeared – it literally was on top of a bunch of papers and keepsakes I had been carting from country to country … house to house … and hadn't looked at for years. I mean YEARS! When I flicked through it, smiling at the memories it conjured up, I saw this note in my grandma's familiar scrawl. I stopped and thought, *wow! So that's where this memory came from.* A simple paragraph – that Grandma Eunice probably meant in a light-hearted way – would shape my personality, my self-esteem, my ambitions for the next 40 years. (However, if I'm truly honest, knowing my grandma – she probably DID mean it!)

In my professional role as an editor and publisher, I've always known how powerful words can be. Every word, particularly in combination, has meaning. They can be hurtful, inspiring, thought-provoking, scary, intimidating, exciting, entertaining, and heart-breaking.

Words are EVERYthing.

Think about it … the parents of a baby are soon asked: 'Has he/she talked yet?'
When the baby is a toddler: 'Can they read yet?'
When the toddler starts school: 'Can they write yet?'

The expectation for speaking and reading and writing is a high priority and basic human function. Like sleeping, eating and drinking. But, I suspect, very little effort goes into training or explaining the power that words have on yourself and others.

I can remember as a child in the schoolyard this ditty being uttered by many, often in a defiant tone: *'Sticks and stones can break my bones, but words will never hurt me'*. Who the heck thought that up anyway?? It certainly has stuck over the generations. And it's so NOT true! I suppose, in one way, you think if you teach your child that mantra, they will grow up believing it and be able to flick off negative comments delivered by uninformed, insensitive people. But what if it means they grow up thinking they can say whatever they want to someone and it doesn't matter because 'words don't hurt'?

Ahhhh, life is so complex.
'Nature versus nurture'
'Do unto others…'
'Be kind…'

Self-esteem is a hidden curse! (Note to self: look up where this word came from as it really pisses me off.) Google 'self esteem quotes' and see how many images that come up. What's your fancy today: positive, cute, sad, inspirational, uplifting, self-confident, celebrity, healthy, happy, motivating … there's a whole industry devoted to teaching you *how to improve your self-esteem*. In other words, how to **like** yourself.

How can one be raised in a happy, stable, fairly normal-functioning 20th century, two-parent family and have self-esteem issues? What if a child is taught that 'liking yourself' is a basic part of being a well-adjusted human? It's not vanity; it's an essential life skill. I was taught many important values – either by nature or by nurture – but our family skipped the part where it was encouraged to like (and be proud of) yourself.

self-esteem

noun

belief and confidence in your own ability and value

Cambridge English Dictionary

So, I go back to my grandma's entry in the autograph book ... why have her words had such a profound (if subconscious) effect on me for 40 years? Yes, I'm the seventh of seven daughters. The number seven does seem to have lucky connotations attached to it. (But, then again, somebody made that up too.)

I've always been driven to achieve. Achieve what? Well, I don't know really ... just achieve 'something'. I honestly can remember thinking over the years, *I have to do something special.* They were my grandma's words – but it was my earworm. Problem is, I never defined what that 'something special' would be. So, here I am, in my fifties, still banging on in my head that I've got to 'achieve' something.

No wonder I have chronic fatigue syndrome.

How about I make a list – would that make the earworm disappear?

- ☑ Happily married
- ☑ Raised children (three + three step-kids)
- ☑ Bought a house (on my own)
- ☑ Dream job in corporate
- ☑ Successful entrepreneur
- ☑ Built a house
- ☑ Travelled extensively
- ☑ Lived in multiple countries
- ☑ Strong family ties
- ☑ Genuine friendships
- ☑ Financially secure
- ☑ Strong values and faith
- ☑ Commitment to community
- ☑ Survived major surgery

That's a pretty solid list, and actually, not even all of it. I should be proud of myself … of what I've achieved. None of this fell in my lap … it was hard work, determination and effort that allowed me to tick these boxes. But the sense of not being fully accomplished – that may have come from this recurring earworm.

I'm such a contradiction! I am not shy of going after goals. But why do I have such a low opinion of my value? Again, being completely truthful here – I'd have to admit that I don't always set my goals very high ... because I'm not confident enough in my own ability. So, if I take this thought-process right back to the very start of the chapter – I cannot trust myself to NOT fail. (*Avoid what you can't control.*) Therefore, my destiny, what I believe in my heart and my head, remains unfulfilled.

Bollocks!

Who wrote that? They are just *words*. Words become thoughts. Thoughts become beliefs. Beliefs become (or stop) achievements.

word

noun

a unit of language that has meaning and can be spoken or written

Cambridge English Dictionary

Grandma Stuart (the surname of her third husband – she had two more!) was my mum's mum. She was a hard woman – with high expectations for her daughters and her granddaughters (and probably herself too). I can see that now. She passed away, bless her, at age 97 – and she was strong, defiant, classy and proud to the very end. My mum? She passed away a few years ago at the age of 93. She was strong, defiant, classy and proud to the very end.

Hmmm ... there's a pattern here.

I know my grandma didn't really come into her own until she hit her sixties. The first time she took a trip to the UK (from Canada) was when she was 60. The last time was when she was 92 – where her fifth husband died while they were on a three-week coach tour of Europe. Can you imagine coping with that in a foreign country at age 92?

Mum started living the life she wanted after she hit 60 too. I know that my six sisters and I got a lot of our strength and determination from our female line. I'm the youngest woman of this third generation – a position I am proud to hold and determined to make memorable.

I'm a huge lover of genealogy. Looking back at our ancestors to see what they went through – to see how their choices affected their future generations – is fascinating to me. It only takes a couple of episodes of 'Who Do You Think You Are' to get hooked on the intrigue and mystery of one's past.

Who defines what your best achievement is anyway? I'm sure many generations grow old, lamenting what they 'could have done', what they 'should have done'. (A nod to my friend Michala Leyland who teaches her clients to 'sod the shoulds'!) It's only when we take the time to delve into our history that we really see the significance of (and appreciate) the accomplishments of our ancestors.

Wow, what a huge breakthrough this has been for me! ***We*** don't choose our significant achievements – history does! All we have to do is 'show up'. Yes, it's important to have goals, to have some idea about what you want to accomplish – but life is constantly throwing curve balls. We can't POSSIBLY map out our life every step of the way. Making a commitment to yourself to 'show up' for every opportunity that presents itself is a helluva goal in itself. Inadequacies, insecurities … they are all a state of mind. They are just nasty 'words' that you think in your head and the person they are hurting is yourself.

The reason I am a dual citizen is because my paternal grandmother was born in the UK. As a young woman, some of her family emigrated to Canada. She had no idea what she was coming to – what would become of her life, what the consequences of her decision would be. I can imagine the fear – leaving behind her parents, and the Norfolk culture to travel on a ship across the Atlantic Ocean to the unknown. What was her motivation? Was it adventure or hope or curiosity? Did she long to experience this vast new country that surely her older brothers wrote home about? Whatever it was that led her to leave behind all that she knew, I can say that she did not have an easy life. I'm sure the undeveloped part of Ontario that she settled in after marrying my grandfather would have seemed unbelievably primitive to her English roots.

However, her choices laid the path for my future – and my children's future. I am quite sure that Grandma Alice did not view her life as anything extraordinary. She died before I was born, so I never knew this woman who 'showed up' when opportunity called to come to Canada. But because of her choices, I was able to have the opportunity to also cross the Atlantic (albeit on an aeroplane) and experience life in a new country. I 'showed up'.

As I'm writing this, I begin to see the folly of it all. Self-esteem: is it low? Is it high? Or is it entirely a word meant to make you question yourself, to doubt what you're capable of achieving? To cause you to avoid 'showing up'? I'm beginning to think it's another nasty word that sneaks its way into our unspoken vocabulary very much uninvited at an early age.

You know what, Grandma Eunice? Much good HAS come of my life. And I'm not done yet. Thanks to the brilliant surgeons of Liverpool Heart and Chest Hospital, I'm going to crack on creating a history that I'm sure someone from my future generations will admire. (That story will have to be another chapter one day.)

I'm writing this whilst sitting on my deck with my laptop. There's a warm, sultry breeze and I can hear the waves lapping at the shore a few hundred feet below. The odd shouts of laughter I hear from one of the sailboats dotted on the lake reminds me that someone's having a grand afternoon.

My Canadian and Welsh flags are gently blowing in the breeze from the flagpole that stands proudly in front of our 'other' home: a subtle reminder to visitors that I'm a dual citizen. The clear blue lake stretches out in front of me and into Georgian Bay beyond. It's surrounded on three sides by the stunning Niagara Escarpment with its characteristic white bluffs carved over thousands of years. This is where I was raised. This view is part of my DNA and in fact, the house where my grandma wrote in my autograph book 40 years ago is just across the bay. If the trees hadn't grown so tall, I could see it from my deck.

I'm planning my return journey to the UK in a couple of weeks – where I have another beautiful home with a view of the gorgeous hills of North Wales. My three young-adult kids are there, preparing for their exit into adulthood. How did I do with teaching them about 'liking themselves'? A familiar earworm pops into my head again – this time it's from Meatloaf: 'Two Out of Three Ain't Bad'. I've still got some work to do as a mum – it's not too late. That is, if she'll listen to me. (Yes, I'll give her this book to read!)

It's warm here in late August – so it's sundresses most days. I see the scars from my open-heart surgery on my legs and on my chest. That was only a year ago when I almost didn't make it. I was embarrassed by these scars for many months – but one of my daughters kept telling me that I should be proud of them – they saved my life.

perspective

noun

a particular way of considering something

to think about a situation or problem in a wise and reasonable way

Cambridge English Dictionary

It really is all about perspective. We can choose to see or react to situations in many different ways. Of course, there will always be external factors that will affect our decisions, e.g. job, family circumstances, finances, health … but even with these, we have a certain amount of choice – to either accept, or change. What I'm really talking about though, is those nasty words in our head – the words that make us doubt our ability, our value – our 'self-esteem'. Absolutely we have choices; it just takes guts to make the uncomfortable ones. The more we let these words stay in our head, the more likely the thoughts will rule our decisions, our potential, our *perspective.*

What is so absolutely amazing about life is: adventures and opportunities are endless! Think about it – they are everywhere! It's just choices that either stop or encourage you from taking them. Do you remember the saying, 'when one door closes, a window opens'? It's true – but only if you want to make the effort to crawl through the window.

I know in my heart that everything I've done, I've given 100 percent. Maybe it's in my DNA – from previous generations. Maybe it's because my grandma challenged me to achieve when I was just a child and it stuck with me. Maybe it's because of some other reason that I haven't figured out yet. However, I know that every time I have had an opportunity, I grabbed it. I showed up. (Okay, except that one time I passed on Bolivia.)

I don't know where my thoughts of doubt, of not achieving 'enough' have come from, but I do believe it's time to send them packing. I'm not done showing up, either. Cue another business opportunity that I'm building with my husband and it is going to be flipping amazing!

I won't be around when my great-grandchildren are faced with opportunities and adventures. Maybe one or two of them will be curious enough to look back at my life and be inspired to go on and do great things. Or, at least have the confidence to TRY new things. Maybe it's time I start writing my memoirs – and then let my future generations decide if I fulfilled Grandma Eunice's prophecy or not.

I joke with my kids that on my gravestone I want engraved: 'She Got Shit Done'.

I'm okay with that legacy.

About the Author

Susan Miller is a publisher of independent authors and in her spare (!) time volunteers on the boards of many non-profit organisations.

Sue is the glue that binds many authors' dreams but admits not having taken the time to write her own book – despite having a long list of ideas from a lifetime of ups and downs. Forever putting others' needs before her own, Sue felt that now was the time to tip-toe into the author world herself. She's come to realise that life is just one big story that if shared, can touch or inspire any number of people.

A mum to three young adults, more than anything else, Sue hopes her life's journey will cause her kids to one day say: 'Wow!'

Connect with Sue:

Website: www.teamauthoruk.co.uk
Facebook: @teamauthoruk
Instagram: @teamauthoruk
Twitter: @teamauthoruk
LinkedIn: meetsusanmiller

Meatballs and Manifesting

By Aga Mortlock

'I had to make you feel uncomfortable, otherwise you never would have moved.' ~The Universe

So, here I am on my 26th birthday, sitting in my boss's office, getting sacked.

Fair enough, this wasn't my dream job. Even during my interview when I was asked where I wanted to be in five years' time, I said I wanted to be a professional photographer. In hindsight, this probably wasn't the best response while trying to get a job in a bank but photography was what made my heart sing. To my surprise, I got the job! It was a good gig at a very well-respected bank and being called a 'marketing executive' really tickled my ego.

Being sacked on my birthday wasn't the worst thing that had happened to me at that time though. It's fair to say I felt like I was having a run of bad luck – three months before this my boyfriend had left me. Yeah, things could have been a lot worse (and we've all heard the saying 'there are plenty more fish in the sea'). But I had all my eggs in this basket. The relationship was looking promising and I truly believed we were going somewhere.

My boyfriend had a lovely family, a great job, and was financially contributing towards the upkeep of my flat. Things were going really well, and he was so keen that he moved in with me after only a few weeks of us being together. A few months later, we were talking about buying a plot of land and building our own house.

I was just as keen. I really wanted to show him how much this all meant to me so, as a sign of my everlasting love I decided to learn how to make meatballs. What's so special about meatballs? Well, I am a vegetarian and can't cook to save my life. I am the one who burns water in a kettle!

I was also prepared to give up on my dream of taking my photography to the next level by turning it into a side business. I had already had some photography work published and I knew I was good at it, but my boyfriend had said that it would never make me money and was a waste of time. So, I put my dream to one side and started settling on the idea of one day becoming a good wife, living in the suburbs, having a respectable job and, in the future, raising a bunch of kids.

This is what people do, right? And this is what I thought was good for me.

Sadly, it wasn't to be. As quickly as he was ready to put his toothbrush in my holder, he decided that this was too much for him and went back to live with his parents.

Just like that, all the sandwich making and getting my hands dirty making meatballs was for nothing ... I was devastated.

Fast forward three months and here I was on my birthday, just about scraping myself off the floor, only to be told that I was being made redundant due to staff cuts. I didn't see any of it coming; I guess it was the universe's way of telling me that a normal life wasn't for me.

The next few months were not fun at all.

I had no money to pay the rent, my phone got cut off and I was late with my bills. Getting a job in Poland back then wasn't easy. It was the middle of the winter; it was dark and cold. I felt heartbroken and helpless.

Into the Unknown

I remember one particular night. It was New Year's Day, and I was on the phone with my friends telling them how shit everything was. Everyone who knows me knows that I can be melodramatic at times but that evening it was different. I really felt like this was it. I couldn't see light at the end of this very dark tunnel, and I was about to quit. Whatever that meant. My friends knew that I needed help and I needed it quickly. One of them was living in Manchester at the time and she suggested that I get a ticket and come over for a change of scenery for a while. She didn't have to ask me twice.

I had nothing to lose and nothing to keep me in Poland. Since my mum's death five years earlier, I felt like I had no roots there anymore. My home was gone because she was my home. My dad was trying his best to look after me but he had lots of his own stuff going on. So, I borrowed some money and, on the 23rd of February 2005, I was on a plane with a one-way ticket. I couldn't even afford the return one. I only had £100 which my stepmom had kindly squeezed into my pocket when I was leaving. I landed in Manchester and it felt good. I had no idea why, it just felt like I was meant to be here. Age 26 and starting again, sharing a two-bedroom flat with four other people.

My English skills ... well, I was optimistic at first. I'd had some exposure to American-English back home but when I started my first job in a lovely pub called Britons Protection I hardly understood a word that people were saying. The accent seemed extremely different to what I was used to, and I realised that talking to native English people was very different to attending language classes in Poland.

Obviously, I didn't want to work in a bar for the rest of my life. At first I thought I'd only spend a few months in the UK to get my head around things. Weeks turned into months and I began to enjoy being here. I talked to anyone who would listen about photography and how much I would love to do it for a living, and no one said it was a stupid idea or that I was never going to make it. They were encouraging and supportive. It was a completely different attitude from what I had experienced back home.

I remember there was one guy in particular who was very eager to convince me to stay in the UK and pursue my photography ambitions. Now I know that he had his own agenda. A few years later, he asked me to marry him, and I happily agreed.

Once I had decided that I was going full steam ahead to get a job in photography, opportunities started emerging very quickly. It almost felt like everything was already there waiting for me. I just needed to make the decision and go for it.

The next few years were totally amazing. I shot for fashion magazines, photographed interiors and events. I also worked in fantastic studios specialising in portrait, makeover, and family photography. I quickly realised that photographing people was what made me tick. I loved seeing people being excited about what we created; I loved seeing their self-esteem going through the roof because I'd shown them beauty in themselves that they were not expecting.

My confidence grew and eventually I thought, *why not set up my own studio and stop working for others?* But my imposter syndrome kicked in again and I was unsure if I could cope with the logistics, emails, set up, paperwork, admin etc. I felt I needed support.

Generally, if I ask the universe for something, I tend to get it. So, very soon I came across someone who felt like the right person to set up a business with. We were both photographers working for the same portrait studio and it seemed like running something like this on our own made perfect sense. We very quickly put our money together and cracked on.

We picked Liverpool as the location for our new venture. Even though we were based in Manchester this felt like the right move. There weren't any other studios like us in Liverpool – and we all know how glamorous scousers are, right?

We hit the jackpot. For the first few years, we were smashing it. At one point, we were hiring 12 staff and the money and clients were rolling in. But it was intense. Six days a week and always a 12-hour day at least. We were tired but it felt like it was worth it. It was our baby, our investment, our sweat and tears. We were spending more time together than we were with our partners. Everything revolved around work and, for some time, this felt like the right price to pay for success. I worked hard but I also played hard. I could afford to travel to places I had always dreamt of – Argentina, Brazil, Peru, Chile, USA, Canada, Barbados, Thailand, to name a few. I'd paid for my wedding and redecorated the house.

I was also reaching burnout. I remember sitting in the studio one day editing images. I was looking at my Mac, wanting to go online but unable to remember which icon on the screen I had to click. My mind was blank. I was forgetting words, putting keys in the fridge…

I knew things weren't right so I went to the doctor and he said my symptoms could be one of two things: a brain tumour or exhaustion. After a CT scan and a nervous two weeks of waiting for the results, the scan was clear. Option B, then: exhaustion.

I was approaching forty. I seriously needed to think about what I wanted next for myself and my family life. Did I want to be a mum? Or did I want to continue to work, albeit at a slower pace, and travel to the most amazing places on the planet? I had options but I was getting on a bit, so like it or not, it was decision-time. It wasn't an obvious choice; I wasn't one hundred percent sure if being a mum was for me but I also wanted to give it a go.

I guess it *was* for me as Harry arrived three weeks early on 27th December 2017 by elective C-section. I went for a routine check-up scan and was told that my baby was too small and that they had to get him out earlier. I was panicking! I was so busy at work that I hadn't bought a thing for the baby. I thought I still had time to go shopping. I also felt guilty for going on maternity leave two days earlier than I was supposed to. Totally ridiculous, I know.

But this was exactly where I was mentally. Dedicated to my work.

Six weeks after giving birth I was back at the studio doing a couple of days a week since we were short-staffed. I was pumping milk in the toilet, feeling exhausted and often on the verge of crying. I felt guilty when I was working because I wasn't with Harry. I felt guilty when I was with Harry and not giving 100 percent at work. It was a vicious cycle.

People often say that you can't have it all. Well, you can have an amazing career and be a mum. But it helps to be in the right job to have it all. You need to become a queen of logistics and work around you and your family, otherwise you'll burn out. Something's got to give.

I went on autopilot, trying to cope with work, looking after the baby, and commuting from Manchester to Liverpool because that's what you do. You don't give up on something you've created even if this doesn't serve you anymore, right? I felt like I had to carry on despite the fact that my heart wasn't in it anymore.

Deep down I knew I was done but I was too frightened to leave what I had worked so hard for.

But the universe was listening as always and delivered what I needed (even if I didn't realise it at the time).

Where Change Begins

In August 2019, I was sitting on my couch at home feeling like someone had pulled a rug from underneath my feet. My business partner had just left after a brief conversation. She announced that she wanted to go her separate way; just like that, out of the blue. Fair enough, the working relationship between us was tense – I couldn't give as much at work due to my new circumstances – but I never expected things to turn out like this;. no talking the situation over, no preparation, no discussions.

The options were: I was buying her out or she was buying me out. I felt let down, betrayed, heartbroken … Scared.

I knew straight away that buying her out wasn't an option. A studio-based career wasn't for me anymore.

So, here I was forty-one, petrified, and starting over AGAIN…

After a few days of feeling angry, despair and lots of other things that you feel when you've been dragged out of your comfort zone, I decided to create a plan of action.

There were a million questions in my head. What kind of photography was I going to do? Which direction should I take? How would I get started? How would I build my client base? So as you do, I Googled it! This is the logical course of action if you need advice about anything in life, obviously…

Before long, I had written down all the steps that I needed to create a business. How to register with Companies House, how to design a logo, where to get a website, networking … the list goes on.

It was time to crack on.

I remember going to my first networking event on my own with my sparkly brand-new business cards. I was seriously thinking, *what am I doing? How is this going to work? How am I supposed to start talking to strangers about my business and myself?* Cringe! But I went. I started chatting to people and guess what ... I WAS TOTALLY FINE!

The next few months were incredible. I met so many new people, fantastic entrepreneurs and business owners. I started taking first bookings and everything was going from strength to strength. I had found my niche – personal brand photography. I knew by then that I wanted to work with entrepreneurs and help them to elevate their business by creating show-stopping images for their brands. Images they would be proud of, that would boost their confidence and skyrocket their marketing.

By February, I had my diary fully booked and I was in full swing. I was so happy and thankful and loving everything about my new business. I was on top of the world.

And then ... March 2020 happened. Welcome to a world pandemic!

Seriously?! I was thinking to myself, *I have just started and I am supposed to shut everything down, go back into my hole and hide?* NOT THIS TIME!

This wasn't an option. I couldn't give up. Not after all the time and effort I had spent rebuilding myself and my business. Thankfully, I was surrounded by fantastic, open-minded people who were like me.

People who wanted to carry on despite the drama which was unveiling around us.

I was prepared to try everything to keep my business afloat and keep serving my clients despite the lockdown. This is how virtual shoots came along. I, along with a few other photographers, discovered a way to photograph people in their homes using Facetime and Zoom. There were so many people who, like me, wanted to fight for their businesses and keep their marketing going. People were moving their businesses online and needed content and visuals to portray their brands.

Virtual shots were an instant hit and kept me busy for the first lockdown. When we opened up again, I found I was taking bookings for face-to-face brand shoots with a lot of my virtual clients. My business was back on track! I had managed to keep visible, I kept in touch with my network, and I kept building my relationships and connections.

I met incredible people along the way, people who built me up, believed in me, loved me, and cheered for me. People who shared their passion and insecurities with me and trusted me to help them create businesses of their dreams.

Now I am an expert in brand photography and travel across the country to photograph the most amazing entrepreneurs who are true inspirations. We often become friends and they become part of my life.

And guess what? I'm not stopping here. There are many amazing adventures on the horizon and so many new ideas. I'm excited to keep building what is my passion and true purpose.

So here I am today, thinking about all those situations and people who led me to where I am now. Especially those which really challenged me, made me get out of my comfort zone, tested my limits, and made me cry.

And I couldn't be more thankful.

P.S. I have even given up on making meatballs.

About the Author

Aga Mortlock is a professional brand photographer, specialising in creating high-end, natural and engaging brand visuals that boost your profile and take your business to another level.

Aga has a unique ability to put people at ease and an eye for creating natural shots that showcase your brand and give your self-confidence a boost. Her mission is to make photoshoots fun – an experience that's quite life-changing for her clients.

Aga is based in Hale, Cheshire, and travels across the UK and Europe to photograph entrepreneurs and business owners, creating outstanding images that reflect who they are and tell their brand story.

Connect With Aga:

Website: www.agamortlockphotography.co.uk
Facebook: www.facebook.com/agamortlockbrandphotographer
Instagram: www.instagram.com/aga_mortlock_photog
LinkedIn: linkedin.com/in/aga-mortlock

About the Host

Katherine Massey is the *Visibility and Confidence Queen,* a business consultant facilitating powerful networking connections and visibility opportunities for entrepreneurial women. She retired from her 26-year career in 2017 to write her memoirs *Living With Dolls: A Story of Love, Mental Health and Freedom* (published in 2018). As a mental health advocate, she helps and inspires others through sharing her own life experiences.

As the host of *Seen - Volume 1* - Katherine has realised another of her ambitions - to encourage women to recognise the power their stories have to inspire others who may feel isolated in the vulnerability of mental health struggles. Katherine has learnt to be 'seen' herself in the press and on TV on many occasions. She knows that being visible, speaking out and sharing her story has helped many. Creating a platform to help other women be 'visible' has been a dream come true.

Connect with Katherine:

Website: www.visibility-queen.co.uk
Instagram: www.instagram.com/visibilityqueenkat

Acknowledgements

To each co-author that trusted me with their words, to be seen and leave their legacy within these pages.

To Sue Miller, founder of Team Author UK and *Seen* co-author, for giving me the confidence to believe I could host a book collaboration like this.

To Michelle Catanach for her professional, calm and experienced execution, from the beginning brief to delivering more than I ever expected.

To Michelle and Christian Ewen (Write On Time Ltd), my VQ Academy membership PR associates, who have delivered exceptional training and support for the launch of this book to get the very best it deserves.

To author and podcaster Karen Kelly who has supported and encouraged our visibility.

To Alice Oliver, TV presenter and podcaster, for her continued support.

My deepest gratitude to you all.